THE MIRACLE OF

POWER

*The New Way to
Riches, Love, and Happiness*

THE MIRACLE OF PSYCHO-COMMAND POWER

The New Way to Riches, Love, and Happiness

by

Scott Reed

Parker Publishing Co., Inc.   *West Nyack, N. Y.*

Printed in the United States of America
ISBN 0-13-585679-5
B & P

This book is respectfully
dedicated to my uncle

SAM M. NICENHOLTZ

who has supplied me with much of the knowledge
and insight that went into it, whose wit, wisdom, and
maturity I came to depend on, and in whom I have
always been able to confide.

HOW PSYCHO-COMMAND POWER BRINGS ANY DESIRE EASILY AND AUTOMATICALLY!

Psycho-Command can change your life instantly—from the very moment you let it work for you!

Regardless of your age, circumstances, or personal problems, this tested method can start helping you now—easily and automatically—to enjoy a richer, fuller, happier life. Its purpose is to bring you *more* of every good thing—money, love, power, friends, new wisdom, spiritual healing, and much more.

As you sit reading this now, wondering how you are ever going to realize those dreams you have, how you are ever going to lay your hands on the money you need, how you are ever going to avoid the misfortune that you have reason to believe is in store for you (or do this for a friend or relative) . . . *there is a way.*

It is called Psycho-Command Power!

STARTING INSTANTLY IT CAN BRING YOU MONEY . . . LOVE . . . POWER!

Psycho-Command means, literally, "mind command" power. It is an actual *materialization method* so powerful it can automatically make the things you desire appear in your life— seemingly out of thin air! It can start working immediately for you, because it has already worked for many others. If it's humanly possible, Psycho-Command can do it for you. It can bring you anything you desire! Anything! Easily and automatically like savings in a Cosmic bank account! It can

* Materialize all your fondest dreams—make your dreams come true!
* Double your wealth and keep it doubling—endlessly and automatically!
* Bring you something for nothing!
* Bring your mate to you without asking!
* Make the man or woman of your dreams suddenly appear before you—begging to please you!
* Dissolve all kinds of evil—schemes of others, the cruelty of a neighbor, or spouse!
* Let you see beyond doors—see and hear what others are really doing!
* Make your fortune, in dollars and actual cash, pile up right before your eyes!
* Make any man or woman instantly do your bidding — without uttering a sound or lifting a finger!
* Make others work for you, do favors for you, and actually go out of their way to please you!
* Break through social barriers!
* Let you raise your mental powers and your I.Q. from that of an ordinary person to that of a genius in seconds!

And still that's just the beginning! All this is a proven fact—scientific in every way. Perhaps you do not believe this is possible. But I am going to prove to you that it's true and that *The Miracle of Psycho-Command Power* will work for you!

THE SECRET OF PSYCHO-COMMAND!

For years I dreamed of an automatic way to do things that would make life a heaven on earth. I spent all my spare time in scientific and occult libraries, searching for the secret. My studies ranged from Alchemy to Voodoo and Zoroaster... from Lapland to the Congo... from prehistoric times to our own day. Until one day, it happened!

Late one night, after deep research—and thousands of experiments—into the secret of materialization, *I discovered the Supreme Command for summoning desires out of thin air! I* began saying it, idly, without thinking . . . and as I said it, over and over, a strange thing happened! Call it a premonition . . .

> **The entire room appeared to light up—like light-ning on a dark night! And the object—or person—whatever I desired, seemed to shimmer into view! Seemingly ACTUAL OBJECTS appeared to take shape all around me: money, jewels, riches, fine possessions! MY DREAM OF FORTUNE, LOVE, AND POWER COMING TRUE!**

A strange sequence of events followed, so rapidly that even I am at a loss to explain exactly what happened. In the days and weeks ahead, everything I asked for I received with this se-cret . . . a new home . . . a new car . . . $10,000 . . . $20,000 . . . $30,000 . . . yes, and more! All problems seemed to dis-solve. I felt a mysterious aura around me . . . a feeling of power!

I PUT THIS SCIENTIFIC DISCOVERY
TO THE TEST!

To me, it was like the miracle of the ages—the discovery of the century—come at last! I found that I actually *could* materi-alize desires—seemingly out of thin air—and make things happen automatically. The basic method of Psycho-Command was born!

With mounting excitement, I began to put this amazing new scientific discovery to the test, showing others how to use the Metaphysical Alchemy Power of the Mind! It worked time after time—every single time!

> **People took command of their own lives. Re-gardless of the human problem, no matter how serious or long-lasting, a healing took place: Money problems dissolved—and in their place, a rising tide of abundance and good fortune! Loneliness gave way to love, new friendships, and a glorious new future! Secret heartaches dissolved.**

THE SUPREME COMMAND proved all powerful! Each new day presented another conquest! Lives took on fresh meaning and purpose! "Psychic" ailments vanished—new strength and energy appeared. As one perfect day followed another, it gradually dawned on me that this actually was heaven on earth!

"I b—— i- m—— a- t- H—— P—— t- r—— b- i- m- m— a- i- t- m— o- t- E—— O- a——"

Into these blanks fit the opening words of THE SUPREME COMMAND, as I discovered it. It is said to be based on the wisdom of the ancient alchemists. Night was said to be the best time for using it, although it was also used during the day. If you knew these words (which I will reveal entirely, in the pages to come), you would have the "key"—the "Open Sesame"—that could actually transform your thoughts into reality, to bring about any event or condition you desire most RIGHT NOW!

POSITIVE PROOF THAT THIS METHOD WILL WORK FOR YOU!

My research continued, and I found that many others have used THE SUPREME COMMAND of Psycho-Command Power to gain their desires quickly—almost overnight—so automatic is the nature of this secret! It gives you amazing instant genius power!

If seeing is believing, how would you like to see your fortune in dollars and actual cash pile up right before your eyes? Or see the man or woman of your dreams appear before you—begging to please you, do favors for you?

You're still a bit skeptical? All right then, here's proof. On nearly every page of this book, I show you how ordinary—and even below average—men and women, no smarter, no luckier or or harder working than you—got what they wanted, easily and automatically. How, in every case, it raised their I.Q. to that of an executive genius in seconds!

$500 APPEARS ON KITCHEN TABLE —SEEMINGLY OUT OF THIN AIR!

Phillip O. had an emergency situation that required a lot of cash quickly. Frantically, he tried friends, neighbors, everyone he knew—even banks and lending institutions. But still, it seemed, he was getting nowhere fast. Finally, in desperation, he sent up THE SUPREME COMMAND with Psycho-Command Power! Then, a short while later . . .

> Staring at the kitchen table—which seemed empty moments before—he noticed an envelope with a thick bulge in it! Tearing it open, he discovered $500, the exact amount he needed—seemingly out of thin air!

What had he done, finally, to receive this money? See Psycho-Command Power # 5 in the section on "Instant Money" for the same method Phillip O. used.

ASK FOR LOVE AND COMPANIONSHIP!

Bradford D. bemoaned the fact that he lived alone. At 35, he was a lonely, miserable bachelor. He began using THE SUPREME COMMAND with Psycho-Command Power, to ask for love and companionship. Soon afterward . . .

> The doorbell suddenly rang, and a beautiful tall blond young woman appeared, who introduced herself as Elizabeth. As in a daze, she followed him . . . and their date was followed by many intimate revelations . . . and many other attractive young ladies who were magnetically attracted to him.

What had he done following his effective use of THE SUPREME COMMAND? See Psycho-Command Power # 8.

FINDS MAILBOX BULGING WITH MONEY!

Bill N.—always behind the eight-ball, with a wife and ten children to support—began to use THE SUPREME COMMAND with Psycho-Command Power. He soon discovered his mailbox was bulging with money. Again and again he tried it, and . . .

Again and again his mailbox was so jammed with
money, he began piling it in stacks on the kitchen
table, reporting totals of $600 ... $700 ... $1,012
... $5,118 ... and more! A steady stream of
money! Seemingly out of thin air!

How did Bill N. unleash this torrent of wealth in his life?
See Psycho-Command Power # 5.

*   *   *   *   *   *

As you can see, THE MIRACLE OF PSYCHO-COMMAND
POWER works! With it, you can ask for anything and expect to
receive it. Instantly your life is changed! Working feverishly
from this evidence, I proceeded to set this method down in
writing—so that anyone can easily understand. The Psycho-
Commands are your specific desires (or, in other words, the
means of attaining them) ... to be used with the Supreme
Command!

AMAZING TECHNIQUE IS EASY TO USE!

Say you have used THE SUPREME COMMAND with
Psycho-Command to bring your mate to you without asking, or
reestablish contact with a long-lost friend or relative. To instantly make him or her do your bidding, you simply use the
appropriate Psycho-Command ... seconds later, this person
agrees with you and obeys you! And you needn't utter a sound
or lift one little finger.

MAKES BOYFRIEND SAY "YES!" INSTEAD OF "NO"

No matter how much he or she may not want to follow
your instructions, they carry them out to a "T" every time.
And nobody will have the faintest idea that you're behind it all.
You alone decide when things should start ... stop ... change
around. You'll see how Jill H. used it to make her boyfriend say
"Yes!" instead of "No" ...how Gloria D. brought her mate to
her without asking ... and much more!

With this secret, your desires actually transmit themselves . . . they reach out, imposing themselves . . . and others accept them as their own . . . They instantly want to please you, do favors for you. They offer you love, friendship, gifts, and more. And your desires may be projected instantly . . . regardless of time or space!

INSTANTLY YOUR LIFE IS CHANGED!

It's true! The amazing miracle of Psycho-Command Power must work for you—because it has already worked for many others just like you. For example, you'll see . . .

* How Dorothy E. used it, and suddenly a wad of dollars—$840 in cash—appeared at her feet!
* How Alma J. used it, and $1,000 bonds appeared—seemingly out of thin air!
* How Peter O. renewed the growth of his hair!
* How Warren W.'s eyesight cleared!
* How Kenneth B. was able to "see through" another poker player's hand to win $100! How Polly V. was able to see what her boyfriend was really doing—many miles away!
* How Harry G. laughingly used a Psycho-Command for money, and a stranger handed him $500!

And still that's just the beginning! With Psycho-Command, you call upon a power that works like a thousand "unseen helpers." It's like having an "astral army"—phantom legions of thousands upon thousands of "invisible helpers" at your beck and call. Do they really exist? Nandor Fodor tells us of photos taken of them in modern times. They have been called many names over the centuries—elves, gnomes, fairies, leprechauns, poltergeists, "little people," mental brownies, and more. The fact is, they really do exist—although they are different than you may have imagined. Learn how to call on them, for any assistance you might need, this new way.

THERE'S A MIRACLE WAITING FOR YOU!

The wonderful new life you will find in this book has already been discovered by thousands of others. It's like an

Instant Fortune Maker—a "push button" system for money, friends, power, secret knowledge, or anything else you desire. As a Metaphysician and Mind Scientist, I can truthfully say that here is a method that really works. Many names have been used to describe it within these pages. Each is descriptive of the same thing, however: Psycho-Command—a method that can release a human power more startling, more effective than anything you have ever seen before!

The main benefit of this incredible new method is that it brings you a speedy solution to any problem immediately—without having to wait hours, days, or weeks! It triggers this power into action instantly!

Here is a Master Plan that can put you on the road to a NEW LIFE . . . filled to the brim with love, friendship, pleasure, wealth, and all the wonderful luxuries of the world . . . in just 10 days! At this very moment, things are starting to turn in your favor. Soon life's golden blessings will start to flow into your hands . . . secret heartaches are dissolving . . . and a thrilling new future is starting to take shape all around you.

This book is your Cosmic bank book – your Cosmic savings account – offering you riches for life, magic words that will help you achieve your desired goals.

—Scott Reed

CONTENTS

17

THE MIRACLE OF

PSYCHO-COMMAND

POWER

The New Way to
Riches, Love, and Happiness

Psycho-Command Power #1

THE MIRACLE OF
PSYCHO-COMMAND POWER:
Secrets of Hypnotic Command!

From radio, newspapers, and television, we have heard of the strange occult practices that others make use of. We have heard how wizards, mystics, and psychic masters have performed seeming miracles of healing, psychic vision, and hypnotic command over others.

> But there has been little explanation of how these things were possible—how ordinary people could use these powers. I am going to show you the magnetic spells, commands, and secret rituals for attaining these things. The miracle of Psycho-Command Power!

Perhaps you do not believe this is possible. But I am going to prove to you that it's true, and that these powers can work for you.

SILENT COMMANDS THAT
MUST BE OBEYED

It has now been proven, beyond a shadow of a doubt, that human behavior can be influenced by remote control. Much of the evidence we have of this has been gathered by Dr. Jose M. R. Delgado, of the Yale School of Medicine.* The method he discovered enables him to control the thoughts, movements, and even feelings of others.

> **With this method—at a distance—he has been able to make subjects do anything he wanted. He reports: "By pushing the right 'button' we could make a (subject) open or shut his eyes, turn his head, move his tongue, flex his limbs. He could be made to yawn, sneeze, hop . . ." One subject, "each time she was stimulated . . . would stop what she was doing . . . turn her head . . . stand up!"†**

Is this Psycho-Command? Yes it is. It is a *mind command* method that can delay a heartbeat, move a finger, bring a word to memory, evoke a sensation. No one can resist it. The method is all-powerful.

Delgado describes a man upon whom this method was used. Each time a button was pressed—by remote control radio— the man was forced to clench his hand into a fist. When asked to resist, the man simply could not do it. "I guess," he admitted, "that your power is stronger than mine."

It is possible—with remote control or Psycho-Command—to control specific functions, such as speech, sight, the flexing of arm and leg muscles—*even emotions*. There have been several studies of remote control radio, or Psycho-Command—among them, one in Norway, by Dr. C. Sem-Jacobsen, who reports being able to make patients laugh hysterically, and even ex-

---

*You may recall, some years ago, magazines, newspapers, and television broadcasts featured pictures of a bold experiment, in Spain. Dr. Delgado entered an arena with a bull bred for fierceness. Armed with only a small radio transmitter, Dr. Delgado awaited the attack. As the animal charged, Delgado pressed a button on the transmitter—and the bull suddenly stopped short. He pressed another button, and the bull turned and quietly walked away.

†Maggie Scarf, "Brain Researcher Jose Delgado Asks—'What Kind of Humans Would We Like to Construct?'," *The New York Times Magazine*, November 15, 1970.

perience sexual stimulation,* by pushing a remote-control button!

SUDDENLY CONFESSES HER SECRET PASSION!

According to the *New York Times* article, Dr. Delgado has been able to control emotions such as love, hate, fear, worry, happiness. For example, he says:

> In humans ... states of arousal and pleasure have been evoked. We have seen this in our own experience. [One subject] was a rather reserved 30-year-old woman. [This method] made her suddenly confess her passionate regard for [the operator] —whom she'd never seen before. She grabbed his hands and kissed them and told him how grateful she was for what he was doing for her. [Afterwards] she was as poised and distant as ever ...

Another time, when this "remote control" method was used, the same thing happened again. Dr. Delgado looks forward to the day "not very far in the future" when this method will be used to treat illnesses such as Parkinson's disease, anxiety, fear, obsessions, and violent behavior, the *Times* article states.

THE HUMAN MIND—A BRAIN-WAVE SENDER OR "POCKET INSTA-COMMANDER"

The point I am trying to make with all these examples is that "there are more things in heaven and earth" than you may have imagined. And it is no more unreasonable to assume that the human mind can project thoughts than that a picture can travel a thousand miles and wind up in a little box.

> With the method I propose, you don't need any special equipment—such as a "push button" remote-control radio transmitter—although I suppose you could call it that, referring to the mental equipment we are all born with, the mind, or the method itself. And you don't need any special "psychic" abilities.

---

*Op. cit.

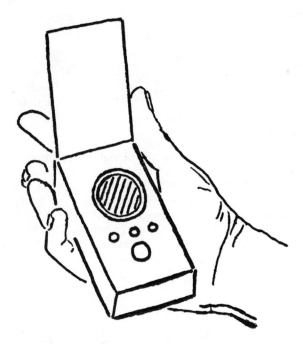

The human mind is a "Psychic Communicator," "Remote-Control Radio," "Pocket Insta-Commander," or "Master Regulator" that lets you broadcast silent or spoken commands that must be obeyed!

Take the strange ability some people seem to possess of hypnotic command over others. Is it really true? Does it depend upon some kind of mechanical instrument or can anyone do it?

Well, we *know* that this can be accomplished by remote-control radio, as Dr. Delgado's experiments, cited above, prove. But what exactly does Dr. Delgado's radio transmitter do? His method is called E. S. B.—Electrical Stimulation of the Brain. And all that his method does is stimulate certain areas of the brain—the individual parts of the brain that make us walk, talk, eat, sleep, love, hate, remember, or forget, to name just a few.

But do you need a radio transmitter to do this—with special electrodes implanted in the brain? *Of course not!* Any scientist, psychologist, doctor, hypnotist—or shrewd observer—can tell you that it is entirely possible to influence others, with similar results, using silent or spoken commands.

Dr. Delgado, himself, admits that his method cannot put thoughts into the minds of others. According to the *Times** article, he says, "Nothing which is not already in the brain can be put there by E. S. B.... Since it doesn't carry specific thoughts ... you couldn't use it to direct a person down to the mailbox to get the mail."

YOUR OWN REMOTE-CONTROL RADIO

But even without Delgado's little black box, *you can* implant ideas in the minds of others. First, there is the simple word command—whether written or spoken—at great distances (by letter or phone) or in person. Ask any person, "Would you please pick up the mail for me?" Or, "Come here." "Sit down." And he or she will do it, in most cases.

Turn up the volume on your own "radio" or "command transmitter"—add a little power—and you get virtually **hypnotic** effects. For example, to quote Reese P. Dubin, in his book *Telecult Power†*:

> ... tell any normal person that he is bright, or handsome, or witty, and he will be greatly taken with this image of himself. In most instances, he will be so busy admiring himself—and thinking that you are admiring him too—that his mind will be clouded to reality [as in a hypnotic trance], much as when a person who is busy talking drives his car through a red light, or walks into a telephone pole. He will absentmindedly agree to things he would not normally agree to—the more so because he is pleased with you for admiring him, and anxious to please you in return. The entire hypnotic process can take place in as little as 10 seconds flat.

Switch a different "button," and you get the same or similar results without words, as both this and Chapters 2, 6, and 8 show. We will have more to say about this in just a few pages.

---

*Ibid.

†Reese P. Dubin, *Telecult Power: The Amazing New Way to Psychic and Occult Wonders* (West Nyack, N.Y.: Parker Publishing Co., Inc., 1970).

The *right* Psycho-Command—whether silent or spoken—will cause any person to do what you desire. This is not to say it should be used to order any person around like a robot, but "remote control" or "hypnotic mind command" does have its uses, since everything you get in life, you get from people—pay raises, promotions, love, favors, friendship, and more.

SECRETS OF HYPNOTIC COMMAND

New power is about to leap into your life . . . an astonishing way to control the thoughts and actions of others without their knowing it . . . No matter how much they may *not* want to follow your instructions, they carry them out to a "T" every time! And nobody will even have the faintest idea that you're behind it all. That's the beauty of Psycho-Command—you, and you alone are the *Master Regulator—you* alone decide when things should start . . . stop . . . change around. Here's how to get started in just 3 minutes.

> In the paragraphs and pages that follow, you will be shown actual hypnotic commands—Psycho-Commands—which you can make to others, through use of the spoken word—in ordinary, everyday life that are guaranteed not only to work, but to prove to you the power of hypnotic command. I call them *Insta-Matic Psycho-Commands or Spells.*

To begin with, you must realize that any idea accepted by the brain is automatically transformed into an action of some sort. It may take seconds or minutes or longer—but ideas always produce a reaction of some sort. Expanding this principle, it can be said that:

> 1. Every suggested idea produces a corresponding physical reaction. Thus, describing to a glutton a succulent dinner, we develop in him gustatory reactions. His digestive juices flow, and he remarks: "My mouth is watering."

2. Every idea constantly repeated ends by being engraved upon the brain, provoking the act which corresponds to that idea. If, in the street, you meet a man who is healthy, strong, and vigorous, and ask him: "What's the matter with you? You are pale; are you ill?", and three or four other suggestions of that nature, he will go home ill.

When you make a suggestion to someone, if he *believes* you, he is in a state of hypnosis. The suggestions may or may not be true, but you have made him think as you wish.

THE MAGIC BOTTLE

Some years ago, a professor at the University of Wyoming appeared before his students, carrying a bottle carefully wrapped in paper and cotton wadding. The bottle contained plain, ordinary water—but he announced that it contained ammonia. "I want to find out how long it takes for an odor of such intensity to fill the room. Raise your hands, as soon as the smell reaches you." He then took out his watch, placed it on the table—and, unwrapping the bottle with great care, uncorked it suddenly, covering his nose.

Fifteen seconds passed, and already most of the students in the front row had raised their hands. Within 40 seconds, the odor had spread to the back of the classroom, in regular waves, as shown by the hands which were being being raised, one after the other, all over the room. A minute passed, and many of the students in the front row began to feel ill, some running to the back of the room, unable to bear the smell.

The experiment was over! The whole class—perhaps 50 people—had been hypnotized in less than a minute!

What the professor wished to discover was—not the expansive power of the smell (for, indeed, there was no smell)—but the hypnotic power of the spoken word.

HOW TO MAKE OTHERS
BELIEVE YOU

This case also illustrates the tremendous importance of the *manner* of conveying suggestions or remote control commands.* For example, certain facts may be withheld—such as the fact that the bottle contained plain water. You may say that all the professor did was trick the class into believing what he wanted. *Exactly!* That is the essence of hypnotic command—and also what makes it so useful when reasoning, demanding, or pleading won't work.

> **It is necessary to be absolutely serious when making a suggestion you wish to be believed. Remember, the impression you are trying to create is one of truth or reality. For only reality is believable. Any sign of laughter, giggling, or nervousness will completely destroy the desired effect. Take the example just given.**

The suggestion of strong-smelling liquid was delivered firmly and with conviction, as though the professor really believed it. "Gentlemen," he said, "this bottle contains a liquid with a very powerful odor. I am going to uncork it to discover the exact time it takes for an odor of such intensity to fill the room."

As soon as he uncorked the bottle, he quickly drew back and held a handkerchief to his nose. In short, the professor was *acting*.

To use the hypnotic power of words, all that is basically required is that you sound as though you know what you are talking about. (See *The Supreme Command* of self-confidence, Chapter 4.) When you do this, your subject believes in you. He expects something unusual to happen—and it does. He actually hypnotizes himself by what he *believes*—indeed, is actually afraid of the special powers of your secret knowledge. *For the human mind can become so taken with an idea that it can completely blot out reality.*

———————————

*At any distance, by telephone for example.

STRANGE HYPNOTIC POWERS

The things you can do with suggestion are a special example of the Law of Reversibility. You see, ordinarily it is sensation—sight, hearing, taste, touch, and smell—that evoke ideas. But with suggestion (which is simply another name for hypnotism), *it is the idea* that provokes the sensation. This is called **hallucination** when it occurs accidentally—and it is called hypnotism when provoked deliberately.

HOW OBJECTS BECOME INVISIBLE

Suggestion may be positive or negative. It is positive when the person upon whom it is practiced is made to believe in, see, or hear something that does not exist. It is negative when it prevents such a person from perceiving a real situation.

It is possible, for example, to render invisible, even in the waking state, a person or object, or part of a person or object. And if, for example, a person or cigarette is rendered invisible—man, cigarette, and smoke will be invisible to the hypnotized person. But, if the man lights a second cigarette—not affected by the hypnotic command—the hypnotized person will be dumbfounded to see, traveling through the air, a cigarette that smokes itself.

Similarly, the suggestion of movements—or active suggestions—may be positive or negative.

The idea of yawning provokes actual yawning—the simple act of laughing will make others smile or begin to laugh (although they don't know why). The reason—as stated before—is that *every suggested idea* produces a bodily reaction of some sort. The more pleasant and agreeable the idea, the more obvious it becomes (like yawning or laughter). At other times, even if we can't see it, it is felt by the person upon whom the suggestion or command is made. The suggestion of itching—if you continually scratch your head, for example—will produce actual itching in others.

In this manner, through hypnotic influence, it is possible to prevent certain movements. A line may be traced, for example, and the hypnotized person will be quite incapable of passing it. Similarly, this person may be commanded to forget a certain word. He may be told that he cannot lift his hand from a table, or get up from a chair, or that his foot is stuck to the floor and that he cannot move it. And he will be quite incapable of doing these things. In every case, *it is simply the idea* of the impossibility that makes it impossible. If you repeatedly suggest that it is impossible, before asking a person to do something, he is bound to feel at least some hesitation.

Through simple suggestion, the actual sensation of heat or cold may be produced. Through simple suggestion, it is possible to diminish or increase the pulse-rate, the secretions; to create ravenous hunger, to satisfy it for several hours (without food); to determine the duration of sleep, to cure insomnia—and much more.

THE SECRET OF SPEED HYPNOSIS

The secret of speed hypnosis is that emotions—such as pride, anger, grief, suspicion, happiness, or fear—seem to speed up the hypnotic process. Why?

Because they cloud the mind to reality. They turn the person's thoughts inward, toward himself—and while he is so busy thinking about himself, he cannot see, hear, or really think about reality.

In this state—which is really a hypnotic trance—he is more and more open to suggestions, which he will accept as reality—because he cannot see reality. And he will absentmindedly agree to things he would not normally agree to.

SPEED HYPNOSIS MAKES HER SAY "YES" INSTEAD OF "NO"

Here is an example of how an appeal to a woman's emotions made her change her mind quickly.

A friend of mine, Joseph X., once told me how he and his wife were able to sell their apartment quickly, to a woman who actually didn't like it, and was insulting about it.

My friend and his wife decided to turn the tables on her by implying that she didn't have the money. In fact, they told her in as many words that they doubted her check was any good. Then, in hushed silence, they just stood there, glaring at her.

This immediately turned the woman's thoughts inward, toward herself. She had her pride to think about—and that is exactly what my friend wanted her to do. It was an appeal to her pride, her sense of dignity and importance. (In effect, she had been told she was really an unimportant nobody.) With rising emotion, indignation, and embarrassment—and a desire to prove that she *could* afford it if she wanted to—she promptly changed her mind (forgetting that she really didn't want the apartment) and signed on the dotted line!

This is a trick often used by salespeople. I'm sure that at some time in the past, you have purchased something that you had no use for. This is the principle that was at work, causing you to make the purchase.

SPEED HYPNOSIS BRINGS MATE
WITHOUT ASKING

Or take the case of Gloria D., whose husband had not looked at her in years. He would fall asleep immediately after supper, or read the papers, or watch television. At first, Gloria thought it was hopeless, but then, after using *The Supreme Command*, self-confidence, she began to formulate a clever plan.

All Gloria did, to shake him out of his reverie, and make him give her the attention she craved, was to imply that he was not the man he used to be. She pointed out how rapidly he had aged in just a few years, his thinning hair, his wrinkles, his "old man's paunch." In other words, she appealed to his pride.

It had a magical effect. "I'm every bit the man I used to be," he snapped! "I'm in better shape now than men half my age!"

Gloria just yawned, "Ho-hum."

That did it! The effect was instantaneous. In the days and weeks that followed, he literally swept her off her feet. No more beer and TV. It was nightclubs, parties, dancing, and more. It was gifts and sweet nothings whispered in her ear. A whirlwind romance began all over again!

SPEED HYPNOSIS WORKS EVERY TIME

When used correctly, speed hypnosis works every time, on all people, in practically every situation. It is the **exact same method** used by professional hypnotists on television, for example, when they apparently hypnotize total strangers in 10 seconds flat.

By first making simple commands—commands that we all respond to, such as the description of food or bodily sensations like warmth, cold, illness, or the impossibility of doing something—he demonstrates to the audience the power of the spoken word. He may take a lemon, for example, and repeatedly describe the bitter, sour, pungent taste of it, until he knows his listeners' mouths are watering. Then he tells them this is happening.

In an audience of several hundred people, when they see these things happening to themselves, as well as others, they become—not only impressed with the power of the spoken word—but fearful of it, fearful of their own seeming weakness and vulnerability, fearful of the hypnotist's special powers.

It is for this very reason that a good hypnotist—a professional stage or TV performer—does not fear large audiences. He welcomes them. The more people, the better. Among them, he knows, there are some who will quickly respond to his commands—more quickly than others*—and the rest, by watching, will also begin to believe in this power. At this point, he selects members of the audience to come on stage—and once again, fear is the operating force.

To the fear of the hypnotist's secret knowledge—real or imagined—and the dread of their own seeming weakness, is

---

*Contrary to popular belief, psychologists say that the more suggestible a person is, the more imaginative he is—and the more imaginative, the more intelligent.

added a very common, ordinary fear called stage fright. Every actor—even the greatest and most experienced—admits to it. The multitude of silent, staring faces poses a danger, real or imagined, that the person will make a fool of himself in some way. Even small children experience this when called upon to recite in front of the class.

The heart pounds, the blood races, the hands and feet tremble and feel cold and clammy. All thoughts are turned inward, toward one's self—and the person thinks, "Why am I acting this way? I can't control myself." He cannot see, hear, or really think about reality because he is so busy thinking about himself. And he is so afraid of what might happen, that he is ready to believe almost anything the hypnotist tells him is happening.

The more he believes, the deeper the trance becomes. In the deepest stage, he can be made to believe in or do anything the operator desires.*

MAN BARKS LIKE DOG

One witness† reports seeing a man put into a trance and told by the operator that he was a dog. The man accepted this, and played the role of a dog to the best of his ability, lapping up milk from a plate, barking like a dog, etc. In another instance, two medical students were hypnotized. One was given soap shavings; he was told it was a banana and that he would relish it, digest it, and feel good afterwards. He ate the soap shavings and had no stomach distress.

---

*You cannot be hypnotized by another, however, if you make certain to convey to your deep, inner mind, the idea that no one can hypnotize you without your consent. In one case, for example, a New York lawyer hypnotized a young girl and repeatedly suggested to her that she should disrobe—in front of 12 other people. She refused to cooperate in any way—and he was astounded at her stubborn resistance. The words of protection she had used prior to the hypnotic experiment were: "I will do absolutely nothing contrary to my moral or religious code. My subconscious accepts this."

†Dr. Joseph Murphy, *Psychic Perception: The Magic of Extrasensory Power* (West Nyack, N. Y.: Parker Publishing Co., Inc., 1971).

GIRL GETS DRUNK AFTER
DRINKING PLAIN WATER

A girl named Mary was given a glass of water and told it was Irish whiskey. She became highly intoxicated, murmuring gibberish and staggering all over the place. Then she was given a tablespoonful of water and told it was a miracle drug which would instantly bring about sobriety and peace of mind. The hypnotist's mere suggestion acted as the perfect antidote—and she awakened absolutely normal and at peace.

*   *   *   *   *   *

Often the hypnotist's reputation is so great—or he looks and acts so sure of himself, so professional—that these three fears (fear of his secret knowledge, the person's fear of his own weakness, and stage-fright) are all that are required, and no preliminaries (such as simple commands) are needed.

HYPNOTIC COMMAND CAN WORK
IN ORDINARY, EVERYDAY LIFE!

Here is a variation of this method—a very simple one—which you may use in ordinary, everyday life. It is guaranteed to work in most situations, especially with friends. The reason I say "most situations" is that, whenever a person is determined to do you harm—and even has friends who are helping him—other strategies, revealed elsewhere in this book, are needed. They, too, are based on the same hypnotic method and are guaranteed to work.

But for now, we will assume the person has no malice toward you—he may even be a good friend. We will also assume that you want something from this person, and he has stubbornly refused—although he has no particular desire to hurt you. Or perhaps you have never even mentioned what you want, but assumed the answer to be no.

The method—although it sounds drastic, but is really quite harmless—is to deliberately make this person angry at you. Insist that he give you what you want. Or, if you have never mentioned your desire, do something else to arouse his anger—act clumsy, for example, "accidentally on purpose." When the person's anger reaches its height—suddenly, without warning—act surprised, as if you had no idea he felt this way.

Let him know that you are hurt, and deeply disappointed in him. Say that you gave him credit for being more intelligent, but that you must have been mistaken. Say that you always admired him—or her—but you see now you were wrong. Then shake your head and start to leave.

When he begins to realize that he has hurt you, perhaps worse than he meant to, he will quickly try to make amends. He—or she—will not want to lose your good opinion (especially if you are of the opposite sex). You therefore use his need to apologize to control him. It is at this stage—his need to make amends—that he will readily grant you many favors. And if you have never asked before, now is the time to do so, for your request is most likely to be granted.

GETS HER MAN WITH SPEED HYPNOSIS
(How to Make Someone More Affectionate)

Evelyn C. was deeply attracted to a man who seemed cold and distant toward her. She had no evidence that he actually disliked her—indeed, there were times when he seemed quite warm . . . and friendly—but, for the most part, he simply acted as though she did not exist. Occasionally, he even seemed to be laughing at her. Using the Supreme Command of self-confidence . . . .

Evelyn decided that if he was ever going to ask her out, she would have to do something about it. One day, while sorting papers in the outer office—she was a secretary in the same company, although not *his* secretary—Evelyn realized that here was an opportunity to make him notice her, as well as get what she wanted. Immediately, she began making a great deal of noise with the papers she was crumpling up and putting in the waste basket.

Very soon, George, the man she was after, came out of his office and angrily inquired why she had to make so much noise He didn't really wish to hurt her—and Evelyn knew this—but suddenly, without warning, she acted very surprised, as if she had no idea she was annoying him. She raised her eyebrows, her mouth dropped open—and then she started whimpering and acting quite flustered.

"I'm sorry," she said. "I didn't realize I was making so much noise. But I don't know any other way to sort these papers. I don't see why you have to holler at me like that—make a big scene and embarrass me in front of everybody. I didn't mean to do anything wrong. I'm just doing what I'm supposed to do. I always thought you were a *gentleman*—that you were kind and considerate. It just goes to show how wrong you can be!"

She shook her head, with great disappointment, sniffled, and began to hurry away. Now George's eyebrows were raised—and his mouth had dropped open in surprise. He suddenly realized that he had acted quite rudely. He was flustered and embarrassed—and he certainly didn't want to lose her good opinion of him.

"Wait!" he called after her, quickly trying to make amends. "I—I'm sorry. Please don't run away."

Evelyn stopped, and turned to look at him.

"Please come back. I don't know what got into me." He took her by the arm and led her into his office. "Sit down," he said, leaning against his desk. "I want to apologize. I certainly don't want you to think that this is the way I treat people— especially someone as hard-working and conscientious as you. I'd like to make it up to you. Why don't we have lunch together?"

Evelyn said yes, she guessed it would be all right. And from then on, she and George became the best of friends, and eventually he proposed to her.

GETS AN INVITATION BY HYPNOTIC COMMAND

Cynthia G. felt left out when she was not invited to a neighbor's party. Instead of sulking about it, she decided to *do* something quickly. Using the method revealed on pages 38-39, she confronted this neighbor and told her point-blank that she was highly insulted. She said she couldn't imagine what she had done to deserve this treatment, that she had always liked her, that she was hurt and deeply disappointed in her.

The neighbor quickly tried to make amends, pointing out that she had merely forgotten to call her, and had not meant to offend her. "I wouldn't dream of having the party without you," she told Cynthia. "Of course, you certainly *are* invited. I'll be expecting you."

SPEED HYPNOSIS MAKES NEIGHBOR PAY DEBT

Speed hypnosis—and the hypnotic effect of emotions—never fail to do their job. I am reminded of the case of James T., who used this method to make a neighbor pay a debt long owed. All he had to do was point out the fearful consequences of not paying the $300. He pointed out that people have had their houses auctioned off for much less. One man, for example, lost his entire fortune, simply because he would not pay $90 on a defective power tool. The store confiscated his property—worth many thousands of dollars more—just to get their $90.

When James T. finished reciting the things that could happen, if he took this man to court, the man—by this time desperate to avoid a legal showdown—said:

"Hold it! Hold it! Hold on a minute there! No need to make a Federal case out of it. Here, look, I tell you what I'll do. I'll make out a check for the amount you say I owe you, and we'll forget about it. Okay?"

THE MIRACLE MAGNET: A Secret That Draws a Tidal Wave of Riches into Your Life!

The power of hypnotic command acts along lines very similar to the action of a giant magnet, *whose great suction pulls to you any person, event, or condition you desire.*

In everything there is a psychic irradiation. The nature of a suggestion, for example, is not the only thing that renders it effectual. There must also exist in the operator a kind of personal magnetism—the result of his practice, of his strong will, of his self-confidence, and of his unwavering expectation of the desired result.

> **This is so true that, where the most educated man can fail to impress anyone with his personality, an illiterate man who has properly managed his gaze, his utterance, and his thought, can easily influence others, and obtain from them the things he desires, with great success.**

Personal magnetism is that quality in man which attracts interest, confidence, friendship, and love. The power of suggestion through personality is like a Miracle Magnet that draws to you any event or condition you wish. And the commands you make are silent commands, like **Insta-Matic Psycho-Commands** or **Spells.**

After a short time, this begins to happen spontaneously, automatically, without any conscious effort on your part.

When you develop personal magnetism, others unconsciously follow your direction, imitate your attitudes, and even copy your style of dressing and speaking!

SECRETS OF SILENT COMMAND

The sending and receiving of thought messages without words is called Telepathy. Thought passes from mind to mind through the great electron sea around us. It is an electrical movement originating in the brain and vibrating the ether. *Thought is not only a dynamic force but is a real thing, as real as any material object.* We cannot smell or taste thought, as we do not smell or taste the pure air. Thought sends out vibrations as light and heat do, but they are of a higher intensity.

> **The chief usefulness of this science is that thoughts may be projected instantly, regardless of time or space. The inborn ability of each and every**

one of us to do this is like a Mental Telephone or
Thought-Wave Sender.

When you have grasped the real significance of the Law of
Mental Control, you will have no desire to parade your knowledge for the amusement of others. You should never trifle with
the mighty forces or exhibit them to satisfy the vulgar curiosity
of others. On the other hand, you should keep continuously
practicing, with the firm understanding that you are paving a
way to a higher use of your growing power.

OBEYING HER SILENT COMMANDS—HE WALKS
ACROSS ROOM AND INTRODUCES HIMSELF

"I gazed into his eyes, and silently commanded him to walk
across the room, introduce himself, and ask if he could be my
friend.

"**I nearly fell over when he started to follow my
silent Psycho-Commands! This was the first time I
ever tried this power. In the days, weeks, and
months ahead, he showered me with money, gifts,
favors, and more. Today we are married, and our life
together is like heaven on earth!**"

"Yet it always amazes me how easily he can be made to act
according to my silent wishes." These are the words of Estelle
W., reporting on the power of silent commands (revealed here
and in Chapters 2, 6, and 8) and the hypnotic gaze.

HOW TO USE THE MAGNETIC GAZE
(Your Desire Magnifier)

The eye is an all-important factor in influencing people. It
not only seems to hold the attention of the person to whom
you are talking, but it is also a power in impressing your will
upon another. The eye of the man, or woman, who has mas-
tered the laws of mental magnetism is a powerful weapon. You
have heard of the power of the human eye over wild beasts and
savages. Here are some exercises which will aid you in acquiring

that magnetic gaze. This is a most interesting study, and you will have the pleasure of seeing the increase of the power of your eyes on people, when they become restless and uneasy beneath your gaze, or perhaps even show fear if you concentrate you gaze upon them for a few seconds.

LESSON 1.

The Mirror Exercise. Place a small mirror on a table before you, or stand before a large mirror with your face about 15 inches from it. Make a little dot with ink on the root of your nose directly between the eyes. Fix your eyes steadily upon the dot, in the mirror, and gaze at it firmly without winking. When you feel impelled to wink, simply raise the lids a little instead and you will have perfect relief. Practice this until you can gaze at the mirror without winking for 15 seconds at a time.

LESSON 2.

The Cardboard Exercise. Take a piece of white cardboard about 6 inches square, draw upon it a circle about the size of a quarter, and fill the circle with black ink. Tape this piece of cardboard to a wall.

Now stand erect, facing the cardboard at a distance of 3 feet, with the spot directly in front of your eyes. Fix your gaze upon the spot and then move your head around in a circle, keeping your gaze fixed upon the spot.

This exercise strengthens both the eyes and the intensity of the gaze. Use it mildly at first and avoid tiring the eyes. Continue this until you are able to gaze for 15 seconds at a time without winking.

LESSON 3.

Circular Influence. Stand with your back against one wall, and—facing the opposite wall—shift your gaze rapidly from one point of the wall to another: right, left, up, down, zig-zag, circle, etc. Over a period of time, the exercise should be lengthened from one to five minutes.

HE TURNS THEIR LAUGHTER
INTO POWER

Martin B. studied the techniques of Miracle Magnetism, and used them with great success in his personal life. As a salesclerk, he had been a dismal failure. He had developed an inferiority complex that prevented him from succeeding. He stuttered and stammered—and even the other salesclerks made fun of him. With Miracle Magnetism, however, he found it was possible to let his eyes speak for him.

His stammering and nervousness soon came under control—and he began to advance even beyond his own wildest expectations. Finally the time came, however, when there was an opportunity for him to become manager of his department. The president of the company had decided to call a meeting of all the salesmen, to get a better idea of who was qualified for the job.

All the old fears came back. Martin was worried sick. He no longer had any confidence. He wanted to avoid the meeting— but he couldn't. To master one person, yes—perhaps even two or three. *But a whole roomful of people*? How? On the morning of the meeting, with a pounding heart, he entered the meeting room and took his place.

When his turn came to stand up and speak, his knees turned to putty. He was shaking violently, and his stammering speech was worse than ever. The audience began to chuckle as he tried to describe his job. Then they began to laugh out loud at his stuttering and nervous appearance.

Suddenly Martin became very angry. He saw his whole life sliding down the drain—all his work, all his effort, for nothing. Just because a bunch of rude people were laughing at him, the job would probably go to some younger man who hadn't a tenth of his experience. He wanted to lash out at each and every scoffer in the room. But he knew that if he tried, his emotions would get the better of him . . . he'd stutter and that would only make them laugh more. In that instant, he knew what he had to do and that he *could* do it.

In dead silence, he just stood there, letting his gaze sweep over the audience, sizing up each and every person, with steel-cold eyes. The laughter died down. One by one, they became uneasy beneath his gaze. Several people who had been laughing were heard to clear their throats, nervously.

After several moments of stony silence, Martin began to speak. In a slow, calm, deliberate voice, he began giving his recommendations for improving the department. Many of these recommendations, he knew, would prove embarrassing to people seated in the audience, because it would become obvious that they had been shirking their jobs.

Martin finished enumerating his suggestions—and then, folding his notes, he looked up at the audience. "You people," he began slowly, "have been very rude to me. And I can't help thinking how really frightened and insecure you must be. In all the years I've worked here, I've done my share—without complaining. I've lent a hand to people who would just as soon spit in my face. I've tried to be a friend. You ought to be ashamed of yourselves."

He sat down in silence, and shortly after the meeting was adjourned, he was summoned to the president's office. "I was very impressed with the way you handled yourself at that meeting," the president said. "I've decided that the manager's job is yours."

Martin left the president's office with a new feeling of self-confidence. Now the tables were turned, he thought. Now those jokesters would find that they had to look up to the one they were always ridiculing. They'd soon find out.

But even before the announcement of Martin's appointment was made, he began to discover the far-reaching effects of the psychic power control he had displayed at the meeting. One by one, a good number of those present at the meeting came to him, apologized for their behavior, and asked him to forgive them. Still others, who had shunned him before, went out of their way to please him.

*   *   *   *   *   *

Use the hypnotic gaze every chance you get. In conversation, look at the person to whom you are speaking quietly and steadily. Think *your thoughts as well as speak them. Never look at anything or anybody in a shallow manner, without having some dominant thought or idea in mind. There is nothing which will disconcert a courteous or discourteous liar more than a* steady look.

In personal magnetism, you look with a purpose—to convey your intention and will. The wandering eye, the blinking, winking, or irresolute eye never accomplishes anything. When looking with a steady and quiet gaze, *think*, picture to yourself a scene, incident, phrase, or sentence. Should the person looked at give expression to the idea or words induced by you, repeat the process again and again with this person, as often as possible, for it means that your influence over him (or her) is increasing.

YOUR SPEED-O-MATIC DESIRE-BRINGER

Having gone so far in the cultivation of the gaze, commence to use it for some purpose. If you should find yourself sitting behind someone, for example, look steadily at the nape of the neck of this person, willing him (or her) to turn around. This can be done, through perseverance.

1. On a train or bus, select a person who is sitting in front of you, and draw a mental picture of a dot in the center of a circle—an imaginary bull's-eye target—on the back of his neck. If your willpower is sufficiently developed, the person will eventually rub the spot you have been concentrating on or actually turn around.

2. When your eyes meet those of another person, direct the magnetic gaze (see pp. 43-44) at him. If he is smiling, will that he frown. If he is frowning, will that he smile.

3. Select a friend and firmly will that he or she perform a certain action—for example, enter a room, go towards a table, take a book, or whatever. Watch your friend intently (or think about him)—and will that he *must* do it, if not immediately at least some time afterward. Do this for five full minutes. Then forget about it. Erase it from your mind. And you will find, to your surprise—when you least expect it—that the thing you have commanded will actually happen!

Note: *The above experiment should be tried only at short range, with someone you normally see a great deal during the day—a husband, wife, or business associate.*

COMMANDING AT A DISTANCE OF UP TO 1,000 MILES

With the aid of telepathy, people even at a distance of thousands of miles can be influenced, easily.

Suppose you wish to have an interview with a stranger, to interest him in your plans. You may influence him as follows: Go into a quiet room and either lie or sit down in an easy chair. Relax your mind and body completely. Shut out all disturbing thoughts, and think intently but calmly of the person you wish to influence. The eyes may be closed and an effort must be made to remain steady and calm. Soon you may get a mental picture of the person. If you have never seen the person before, make the figure mentally without any distinct features. When this stage is attained, repeat mentally what you wish to do and imagine him doing as you wish. Your thought waves will reach him with alarming clarity and swiftness.

SHE HEEDS HIS SILENT CALL
AND VISITS HIM

Laurence S. was a Private in the Army, stationed in Alabama. He was soon due to be shipped overseas, and he wanted desperately to see his girlfriend for the last time. Numerous attempts to telephone her failed, as she was out of town. And although he had a 24-hour pass coming up, there was not nearly enough time to travel clear across country to Seattle, Washington and back.

Using this simple method to project his thoughts, Larry found a quiet place, sat down, and began broadcasting these silent commands.

Almost immediately, Louise, who had been visiting relatives, began receiving faint mental impressions that there was something she had to do. But what? From far away, Larry continued his silent commands. He willed her to come to him. And the impressions Louise was receiving became stronger and stronger. Suddenly, she received a clear mental picture of Larry and what he was saying.

In that instant, she knew what she had to do. As if in a daze, she dropped the cup she was holding, told her friends and relatives there was something she had to do, hurried out of the room, and took the first bus to Alabama—arriving in record time. But when she arrived at the base, he was nowhere to be found. Luckily, one of the men told her he was visiting friends in town. She took a taxi to the address he gave her.

Meanwhile, Larry—who had given up hope—was discussing the matter, sadly, with his relatives, when the doorbell rang. *It was Louise!* Hugging and kissing him with great emotion, she explained that "something" told her to come. "You wanted to see me, didn't you?" she asked. *Wanted?* It was as if she'd appeared out of thin air!

"Yes," he replied. "You don't know how much. In fact, you might even say I willed it!"

"Well, I'm here as you commanded," she laughed. "What is it you desire, Master?"

"I desire you to stop acting silly," he smiled. "Come in and meet the family."

"Yes sir," she giggled, giving him a mock salute.

*   *   *   *   *   *

When you are practicing mental telepathy, be as discreet as possible, lest you arouse scoffers. Never let it be known to people around you that you are trying to influence them to do your bidding. Their skepticism might weaken your faith.

Telepathy—like electricity—needs a sender and a receiver. Doubt (the refusal to receive) acts as a kind of short circuit. For example, it has been observed that one skeptical person can frequently interrupt or block a seance. The Supreme Command of . . .

Faith or confidence is probably the most important factor in sending thoughts. Enthusiasm and earnest expectation are the keys. When you want something done, don't just ask, *command*! Mentally shout it. This very state of mind, commanding, is stronger than even words in getting what you want.

Finally, you must never use this power to hurt other people or project unkind thoughts. It can boomerang. For example, if you dislike someone and think this intensely, he (or she) is apt to receive more or less accurate impressions, with a feeling you are hostile. In this case, the person will never cooperate with you—and may even try to do you harm.

THE POWER OF MIRACLE MAGNETISM

Miracle Magnetism—as we have seen—is a phenomenon that does not even have to depend on words to influence others. It can depend, instead, on the magnetic or neural influence of the dominant individual.

The reality of this influence has been proven, scientifically, with instruments which actually show the magnetic influence of the hands or other parts of the body.

By means of such apparatus we are able to verify that animal magnetism or mesmerism is a reality, and that magnetic force varies according to individuals. Everything appears to indicate that great magnetic force develops in the person who knows how to purify his or her body through healthful living. By healthful living, I mean temperance in all things, simple diet, adequate physical exercise, calmness, and evenness of mind.

> **Magnetism can subdue rebellious or unwilling subjects; it can cause marvels, such as levitation or the raising of heavy bodies into space without material support, the germination and rapid growth of plants, and more.**

All psychic and occult phenomena owe their power to animal magnetism. To its dominion belong mental suggestion (telepathy), clairvoyance (clear sight), certain phenomena of magic, and the mediumistic effects of materialization, table-moving, transport, etc.

Experience teaches that practice develops to an extraordinary extent the force of influence produced by magnetism, and it is well, therefore, to practice as much as possible the *drawing power* of magnetic influence.

To do so, attach one corner of a sheet of paper to a wall at the far end of a room, with a nail or pin. Then practice *thinking intensely that it must follow your hands*. Few indeed are the persons who succeed in evolving sufficient nervous force to attract the paper; but these daily exercises, even if unattended by success, will help magnetize you—or charge you magnetically—until you accumulate sufficient power to project thoughts, and even influence objects without touching them.

The celebrated medium, Daniel Home, could dislodge a book from a shelf at 50 paces, without touching it; the Gurus of India succeed, by mental magnetism, in levitating heavy objects and hastening the growth of plants with an all-powerful gaze.

THE AMAZING POWER YOU NOW POSSESS

With Miracle Magnetism and hypnotic command, the doors of society are thrown open to you, and you will draw friends to you as bees to honey. Even unconsciously you will exude this magnetism, and any party assembled will feel an irresistible urge to turn toward you for advice. They will sense that you are the truly spiritual person they have been looking for, a person of deep knowledge, wisdom, and understanding.

Your enemies will suddenly become true friends; people who have previously looked down on you suddenly want to do things for you. They want you to join their country club, their yacht club, their fraternal organization . . . they automatically want to do favors for you and offer you golden opportunities. They offer you money, better jobs, promotions, pay raises . . . anything and everything.

You can ask for virtually anything and expect to receive it. And you'll be absolutely amazed at the ease with which you'll be able to influence those around you to gain love, admiration, opportunities, and the income you desire.

As you will see, personal magnetism rules the world.

Psycho-Command Power #2

YOUR MENTAL BINOCULARS:
How They Let You See
—Beyond Barriers—
What People Are Really Doing!

Psycho-Command Power #2 rips away the veil of secrecy from other people's actions to show you what they are really doing! It actually increases your power to command and control others by understanding their secret thoughts.

Every day, people you meet send you secret messages—without realizing it—that reveal to you their private thoughts. They send you signs that tell you when you are in the company of someone who is deeply attracted to you—despite what he or she might say. They tell you exactly what to say or do in these cases.

They send you signs to let you know whether they are sincere or if they are just taking advantage of you with their flattery. They warn you—unconsciously—of danger, long before it comes to pass, so that you are able to cool off bad tempers before they blow up. They let you know whether you can confide in them, or if they are not to be trusted and would laugh at you behind your back.

They do this through Body Language—the way they sit, stand, walk, talk—even the wink of an eye, the tap of a finger, a nervous glance. Did you ever wonder, for example . . .

* What does it mean when a man or woman looks at you with narrowed eyes?

* What does it mean when a man or woman stares at you, holds your gaze, and doesn't look away?

* What does it mean when a man or woman glances at you quickly, and repeatedly, out of the corner of his or her eyes?

* What does it mean when a woman or man stands close to you and makes you feel uncomfortable?

* What does it mean when a perfect stranger smiles at you?

* What does it mean when the person you are talking to frowns—even when you've said nothing wrong?

What do all these things—and many more—mean? All day long, you are being literally bombarded with silent messages that come to you from other people in the form of signs—what people say or do—with hidden meaning.

I intend to prove to you now that *Body Language* can reveal to you other people's secret thoughts. It will be like having a secret "Seeing" Device or pair of Magic Mental Binoculars. With the knowledge this chapter gives you, you will, in effect, be able to "tune in"—any time you wish—to find out what people are *really* doing, what they are saying by their actions.

With this method, even a photograph sent by a friend or loved one many miles away can be like a psychic electronic telescope that lets you *really* see up close over great distances.

USE YOUR MENTAL BINOCULARS
TO SEE WHAT PEOPLE ARE REALLY DOING

A recent article in *Life Magazine* reported an incident of a leopard attacking its trainer. According to the report: "The beast's eyes suddenly widened, a sure sign of danger." What happened here? The leopard *telegraphed* its sudden surge of murderous rage. Similarly, a cat's purr tells you of its content-

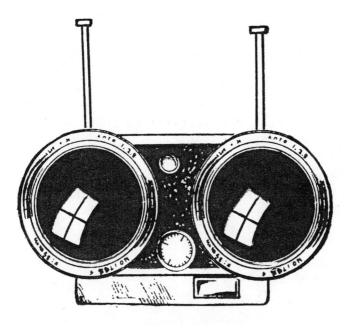

PSYCHIC TELEVIEWER OR
INSTA-VU COMMANDER

*The mind is like a "Secret Seeing Device" (see above) that
lets you see and hear what others are really doing—across a
room, a city, or a continent—through actual physical barriers, such as walls, floors, ceilings, and doors. It likewise
lets you broadcast commands which must be obeyed.*

ment. A lion, intending to charge, signals this by arching his
back.

The point is, people do the same kinds of things. It's easy to
spot them, once you know what to look for. For example, who
has not heard such statements as, "I can always tell when a man
is lying, from the way he tightens up around his mouth." Or,
"You can always tell when John is moody—he picks his finger-
nails." True, not every sign will mean the same thing all the
time. People's moods are as changeable as the clouds in the sky.
But when the *same* sign appears in the *same* situation, time after
time, you can bet your bottom dollar on the meaning of that
sign.

POKER PLAYER USES "SECRET SEEING DEVICE" TO WIN $100

Any poker player can tell you the clues that people give of what they're thinking and feeling. As one such player remarked: "The other day I was in a game with a fellow whose raises had driven everyone else out. We were playing seven-card stud, and he had four hearts showing. Chances were fairly good that he had a fifth heart that would give him a winning flush. That was the way everyone else had him figured. But I stuck to the end, and beat him.

"The poor fellow never knew why I called his bluff. The fact is, I saw that he didn't have the flush. How did I know? Simple! Whenever he bluffed, he tapped on the table with a ring he wore on his right hand."*

SHE TRIED TO TELL HIM BUT HE MISSED THE SIGNS

If you don't pay attention, you may miss these signs, or "silent messages," that other people send you. Most people do. They worry about how they look to the person they're talking to. They want to make a favorable impression. Other times, they're too taken up with their own problems to notice.

There was the case, for example, of the young secretary who wanted to win her boss's attention. Using certain signs revealed in this chapter, she signaled her availability.

He was young, and single, and available—but he was so caught up in his own problems, doing the work of three men, trying to impress *his* boss, that he failed to notice her silent message.

That is an obvious example, but it illustrates the first rule: the more time you spend thinking about yourself, the less successful you'll be at observing and understanding the other person. To see what other people are *really* doing, you must look and listen to *them* and cast your own problems aside.

---

*Reported by Auren Uris, in *The Mastery of People* (Englewood Cliffs, N.J.: Prentice-Hall, Inc., 1964).

HOW PEOPLE REVEAL THEMSELVES

The clues you look for, the symptoms you will spot—using the pictures in this chapter—will help you "read" all kinds of people; those you know very well, those you know slightly, perfect strangers. Have *confidence*. You can and will succeed.

You will discover gestures, mannerisms, movements of the body, what they mean, and how they may even be used to . . .

BROADCAST SILENT COMMANDS

You'll see how certain simple signs enable you to "speak" to someone silently—in the presence of others—without uttering a sound. You'll see how, in certain intimate situations, these "unspoken messages" enable you to express your thoughts— even across a crowded room—without being too bold or forward; to make advances, without taking chances.

There is the case of Roland D., for example, a lady's man, who can walk into a room full of complete strangers and always walk away 10 minutes later with the prettiest, most desirable girl on his arm, without ever having said a word to her.

After his effective use of these "silent commands"—which is, apparently, all she needs to see—a simple "Let's go" is all that is necessary, and she follows, as though hypnotized, by this message. And yet there is nothing special about Roland D. He is not especially good looking. He is no better, no smarter, no luckier than a hundred other men. The secret lies in his knowledge of the "unspoken word."

The same is true of any woman. If she knows the secret, she gets her man—nine times out of ten—through "silent commands."

SILENT COMMANDS BRING $500
IN 10 MINUTES

Some people use Body Language to get what they want, without even realizing what they are doing. A salesman friend of mine, Bill M., for example, swears he didn't even realize it when—through various body signals—he *commanded* an unde-

cided, doubtful customer to buy. He did this by projecting
signals of honesty, sincerity, and enthusiasm to this man. His
silent message was, "I'm only trying to help you." The customer suddenly changed his tune and bought what this salesman
had to offer. Bill made himself $500 in 10 minutes.

TELEGRAPHS HER THOUGHTS
TO THE MAN SHE LIKES

In another instance, a girl named Laura D. "telegraphed"
her thoughts to a man she liked. She didn't realize it but what
she was saying was: *"Please notice me. I like you. I'm attracted
to you. Let's get to know each other better."* The man smiled,
came over, introduced himself. And Laura really got her man
because, as things developed, they were eventually married. But
when I told her that I had seen her message, too—and explained
just what she did—she was surprised.

"SILENT MESSAGE" REVEALS CULPRIT

In still another case, an office worker suspected that someone was stealing valuable documents from his desk, every time
his back was turned, in an effort to make him look bad. The
victim, Harold J., was able to "see" exactly who the culprit was,
through certain unconscious signals this man was sending out.
And by "broadcasting" a silent command of his own, Harold J.
was able to make this man confess what he was doing, and
apologize to the boss for getting Harold into trouble.

Yet Body Language can be made to work for you all the
time—not just accidentally—when you learn the secrets revealed
in this chapter.

WHAT IS BODY LANGUAGE?

Body Language is the way people unconsciously telegraph
their private thoughts by the way they fold their arms, cross
their legs, sit, stand, walk, use their hips, bosom, eyes—even the
subtle way they move their lips.

It is their *unconscious* response to what's going on inside
their minds. People speak and move, and yet only the smallest

part of what they say—just 30-35% of it—is what they're really thinking.

The rest is revealed through Body Language—the way they move—like the twitch of an eye, the tap of a finger, a nervous glance, when somebody has a winning poker hand. Even the way someone writes his name or doodles on a piece of paper can be a giveaway to his innermost thoughts.

How does a man know when a woman is a possible pickup? How does a woman know when a man is flirting? How do we really know if another person means what he is saying? For all of these, there are signs—sometimes not just one, but many.

LIKE A STRIP OF FILM

Three pioneers in the study of Body Language—Dr. Albert E. Scheflen and Dr. Adam Kendon of the Bronx State Hospital, and Dr. Ray Birdwhistell, senior research scientist at the Eastern Pennsylvania Psychiatric Institute and director of the Studies in Human Communication project there—have been examining body motions for the past 20 years.

The method they use is to study actual motion pictures of men and women in common, ordinary, everyday situations, as well as filmed interviews of patients who have come to their clinics for personal counseling. Every bodily movement is studied step-by-step, through the pictures on these strips of film. Each position of the head, brows, chin, eyes, and other parts of the body is studied—regular recurring combinations are noted—and various silent, unspoken, hidden meanings are noted.

In the sequence of pictures on the following pages (which I call a Cyclotron or Psycho-Motion Picture), you will find several illustrations of various body motions, signs, and symbols, that can tell you what people are thinking—and what they are *really* doing.

WHAT THE EYES SAY

Not much goes on inside your head that doesn't show in your eyes. Scientists now agree that what many people have long suspected is true: that merely by watching a person's eyes, you can learn a lot about him or her.

The eyes reveal facts not only about a person's mood, but also about his or her character, health, personality, love life, and much more!

Your eyes always reveal whether you like someone or not—and how much—according to a recent article in *Psychology Today*. Studies at the University of Chicago show that even when we try to conceal our true feelings, our eyes show them. When we meet someone we like, the pupils of the eyes (the small, black dot at the center) automatically widen. The more a man or woman likes someone, the bigger the pupils get. If we dislike someone, the pupils get smaller and smaller.

Fluttering eyelids are often associated with flirtatious gaiety—but research at Washington and Ohio State Universities has shown that the frequency with which a person blinks his eyes indicates how nervous or worried he or she is. And, far from gaiety, the Washington State researchers say that "eyelid flutter is strongly indicative of growing depression."

Scientific studies conducted by Dr. Merle E. Day, of the Veterans Administration, show that when a person is asked a question requiring much thought, his eyes will consistently move in the same direction—always to the right or always to the

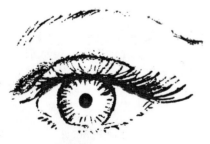

Small pupils mean dislike.

Large pupils show love.

left. (Even in blind people.) Rightward eye-movers were observed to be more outgoing, fun-loving, and gregarious (see Chapter 7, "Passionate" Handwriting, for an interesting comparison—the description is the same).

Leftward eye-movers were observed to be just the opposite —quiet, brooding, introspective, with a tendency to suppress extreme emotion, and to be choosy or selfish about anything that seems important to them. What they say is often not what they feel. Tests showed that eye movement has nothing to do with being right- or left-handed, but rather has something to do with increased activity in the right or left frontal lobes of the brain.

THE "SEXUAL AMAZONS" OR "SECRET LOVER" EYES

There is an area on the lower eyelid, according to Boyce De Mente,* said to be directly related to one's sex life. This area is just below the rim of the eyelid, near the inner corner. Face-readers say that if this area is fleshy and swells up when one smiles, it is a sure sign that he or she has a very active sex life.

The scientific basis for this observation is that this area of the eye is directly linked to the hormonal secretions of several glands. These glands are activated during times of great stress or emotion, such as love, fear, or anger. This area is just below the rim of the eyelid, near the corner, and it swells up during times of great emotional turmoil.

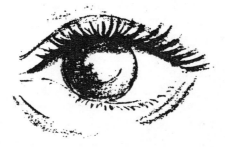

*Boyce De Mente, *Face Reading for Fun and Profit* (West Nyack, N.Y.: Parker Publishing Company, Inc., 1968).

WHAT THE HANDS TELL YOU

Perhaps the most revealing aspect of Body Language is what people do with their hands. If a man says one thing and means something else, his hands can be a dead giveaway. For there are very few movements of the hands that are accidental.

> **Practically all hand movements have hidden meanings. What a person does with his hands, fingers, and arms is directly related to what's going on in his—or her—mind.**

That this is true is no accident. For there is a vast complex of "telephone lines" that link the hands directly to the brain, making them a kind of mental earphone or "listening device" that reveals what another person is thinking. Scientists have observed that there are more nerves between the brain and the hands than any other portion of the body.

The brief descriptions that follow are designed to help you "see at a glance" the secret messages that are being sent to you by other people, with their hands.

Picture #1—Sign of a "Weak Willed" Person

To begin the study of hands, it is necessary to start with clear, simple hand signals, so that later we can see just how these hand signals—combined with other body motions—form complete, silent messages.

The first picture in the series on page 63, Picture #1, is just such a sign. It is a simple one, in which the first two fingers are slightly raised. What does it mean? Simply this . . .

You can tell when someone is about to say something, or wants to say something, by the tendency that many of us have to raise a finger, ever so slightly, as in Picture #1. It is equivalent to starting to say something and then stopping for some reason. Timid people, generally, never get beyond this stage—and aggressive or "pushy" people can often spot this, instantly, as a sign that here is a "weak willed" person that they can push around.

In a game of cards, like poker, for example, or in any business dealing, where one party may secretly have the upper

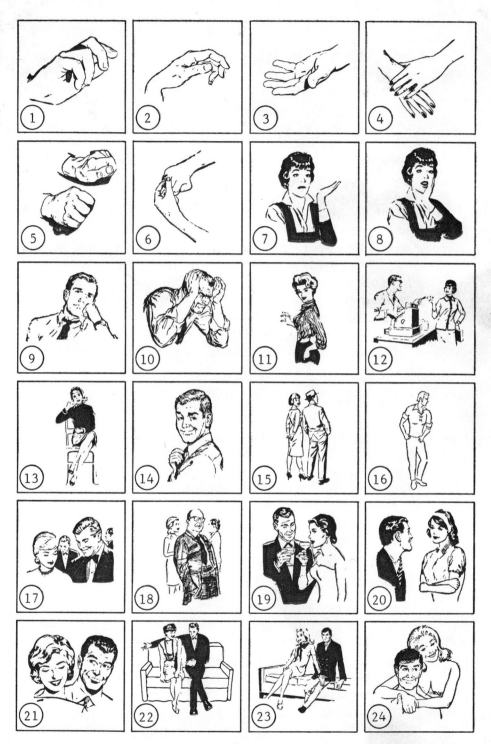

hand—or stands to benefit in some way by remaining silent—this sign can be a dead giveaway. It represents the hidden or suppressed urge many of us have to boast about our cleverness.

Also, the raised finger—or slightly raised finger—is almost universally used as a sign of warning, as if to say, *"Don't do that!"* It is usually used by those in authority, such as a parent, a policeman, an employer, or a supervisor. It is also used in situations involving opposite sexes, where the advances of one are clearly not welcomed by the other. When the sign is not forceful, however—and the finger or hand only slightly raised—it indicates simple fear or uncertainty. The man or woman using this sign, unconsciously, is saying, *"I don't know. I'm not sure."*

Another, more subtle use of the slightly raised finger or hand is among friends, when there is a third party present, and you are saying something—or look like you are about to say something—that may prove injurious or harmful in some way. Then, too, the meaning is clear: *"Pipe down. Don't say that, or you'll get us all in a peck of trouble."*

Picture #2—Boredom or Rebellion

A limp, or hanging hand, has come to signify that a person is bored, restless, or tired. Depending upon the situation, it can also indicate frustration or disgust. It is also the symbol of the dilettante (admirer or lover of the arts), and was formerly used by members of the social elite, during polite conversation. It is believed to have been derived from the position of the hand while holding a pair of opera glasses. It is rarely used today, except unconsciously, to indicate boredom or fatigue, but it can be used in certain situations to indicate contempt, snobbishness, or a desire not to get one's hands dirty.

Picture #3—The Silent Question (Flirting)

A hand held flat, palm upward or outward, has come to symbolize the silent question, *"Why?"*, or *"I don't know. Search me."* But when used by a woman in front of a man, it can have quite a different meaning.

Dr. Albert Scheflen, a pioneer in the study of Body Language, has observed that—whether consciously or unconsciously—women tend to use this as a sign of interest, when courting or flirting.

He says* that ordinarily women show their palms hardly at all, but in courting they "palm all over the place," even smoking or covering a cough with palm out. "From this, you can derive a cheap rule," says Scheflen: "Whenever a woman shows you her palm, she's courting you—whether she knows it or not." (Men do this by combing their hair, straightening their tie, hiking up their belt or socks.)

Picture #4—The Confident Person

You can usually tell a person's mood, simply by looking at his or her hands. If the person is calm, confident, and self-assured, his or her hands will rest easily, moving little. They may simply hang limply at the person's sides, or if he or she is sitting, they will rest gracefully—one over the other—as in Picture #4, or be folded neatly, schoolchild fashion, or finger to finger, thoughtfully. If the person is doing something with his or her hands, such as holding a lit match, the hand will be very steady. With these hand positions, the person says, in effect, *"We are getting along fine,"* or *"I like you,"* or *"I'm completely at ease in your presence,"* or *"I am completely confident that I am correct; that I am doing the right thing in this situation."*

Pictures #5 and 6—The Nervous Person

On the other hand, if the person is uneasy, nervous, or jittery, his or her hands will be quite active. Picking, biting, or sucking the fingers is quite common in such circumstances, indicating tension that must be relieved in some way. Picture #5 shows a pair of clenched hands, which often indicate not only tension, but frustration (the sense of having one's hands "tied") and even anger. Picture #6 shows "ring twisting"—another sign of simple nervous tension. In addition, if there is no ring, it may indicate a sense of guilt as well—such as a married man might feel if he is flirting with someone and has removed his ring. The same is true of women.

---

*Reported by Flora Davis, in *The New York Times Magazine*, ("The Way We Speak Body Language"), May 31, 1970.

Picture #7–Perplexed

Now we come to movements of the hands involving the face and other parts of the body. In Picture #7, the eyebrows are turned up near the center, the mouth in a slight frown. Taken alone, this facial expression would mean, *"I'm worried. I'm afraid."* But with the hand added, it means something else. The person now seems to be saying, *"Why?"*, *"I don't understand!"* *"What should I do?"*—or, *"I'm only trying to help."* Clearly, the addition of the hand has given this expression more depth and new meaning—several in fact.

Picture #8–"Oh, What I Did!" (Embarrassment)

In Picture #8, the eybrows are raised, the mouth is open, the lips are forming the silent word, *"Oh!"* By itself, this face would seem to say, *"Oh, really? I'm surprised."* But with the addition of the hand, placed against the face, it says, *"Oh, what I did!"*, or *"Look what I've done now."*, or *"What have I done now?"*

Picture #9–Contempt or "I Don't Give a Damn"

According to sociologist Erving Goffman,* of the University of Pennsylvania, there are certain very definite things people do with their bodies to express contempt, boredom, or rebellion. These include flatulence, overindulgence, dozing off, belching, spitting, nose picking, scratching, momentary coughing, sighing, yawning, loosening one's belt. He calls these gestures "creature releases."

> **When we see people doing these things, at a party or some other social function, we are—quite correctly—insulted. Our sense of dignity and politeness is offended. And this is exactly what the person doing these things *wants* us to feel. For *"creature releases"* are meant to be direct, outright insults. They are stating, quite boldly, *"You bore me. This party bores me. I don't give a damn. I'll show you what I think of you."***

**Reported by Flora Davis, in *The New York Times Magazine* ("The Way We Speak 'Body Language' "), May 31, 1970.*

But we receive the same type of insults a thousand times a day from other people—without realizing it—because the people sending us these silent messages couch or soften them in a milder, more polite way. Picture #9 shows how this is done. The face is expressionless, except for the mouth, which betrays a slight frown. The face is apparently resting on one hand, which is pressed against the cheek. The picture is one of supreme boredom.

Or the person might hold his hand flat against his forehead, as if to say, "*You're giving me a headache. This is too much.*" We'd be quite insulted if someone sitting amongst us told us outright to shut up. But when he uses one of these "*hidden* creature releases," we simply *sense* that something is wrong, and—as diplomatically as we can—we leave this person alone, which is what he wants.

Picture #10—"Go Away. I'm Fed Up!"

Here, we return again to the direct, bold insult, using silent Body Language. In this particular case, the person is saying, "*Go away!*" or "*I'm fed up!*" To do this, he simply makes a face or turns his face away, and throws up his hands in a gesture meaning "*Go away!*" Of course, direct insults such as these are not taken to heart, and are quite permissible, among good friends. It is when a stranger does these things that the insult is "felt"—and felt deeply.

Pictures #11-13—Female Flirting

According to Dr. Albert Scheflen both men and women show a readiness to court or flirt with one another in certain ways that are similar. First, both men and women show a heightened muscle tone. The individual holds him- or herself erect; legs have tighter tone; and even the face changes—sagging, jowliness, and pouches under the eyes all decrease. Eyes seem brighter and skin may become either flushed or pale. There the similarity ends, and a phenomenon called "preening" begins.

Pictures #11-13 show some of the preening gestures a woman goes through—whether she realizes it or not—when flirting with a man she likes. She will often stroke her hair, check her makeup, rearrange her dress, or push her hair away from her face. She may thrust her breasts forward, place a hand on her hip, or slowly stroke her thigh, or wrist, or palm. She may stand with her head cocked slightly at an angle, one foot behind the other, hips slightly thrust forward. In conversation, she may speak, resting an elbow in the palm of one hand, while holding out her other hand, palm up (an important sign—see comments on Picture #3). Or she may sit in a relaxed position, crossing and uncrossing her legs, slightly exposing one thigh.

Pictures #14-16—Male Flirting

The motions that a man goes through, while flirting, are often so casual that they are often unrecognized, according to Dr. Scheflen. He may comb his hair, button his jacket, adjust his tie, or hike up his belt or socks.

But men who are really attuned to the power of Body Language, and know how to use it effectively, go several steps further. They show their aggressiveness—their magnetism, so to speak—first, by the way they act. Such a man will usually stand with his legs apart, hips thrust forward slightly. He may hook his thumbs in his belt or pockets, hand hanging downward, and walk with a sort of rolling motion, showing an easy grace and self-confidence.

Secondly, men show their aggressiveness by the way they dress, to enhance their appearance and emphasize their good features. If a man has a good body and knows it, he'll usually wear tight or form-fitting clothes that are revealing at the waist, hips, and lower part of the body. If he has a good build, or hairy chest and arms, he may choose to wear an open collar (even halfway down the chest), short-sleeved or even no-sleeved shirts, or he may roll his sleeves up, preferring a tight vest to a jacket. An aggressive man will wear his hair in the latest style—if necessary, attempting to conceal the lack of it, by combing or offsetting it with mustache, beard, and sideburns.

SEX AND THE 5 O'CLOCK SHADOW

According to the British science journal, *Nature*, a Cambridge University scientist has discovered that the rate of growth of a man's beard seems to be directly related to his love interests. A persistent 5 o'clock shadow can mean he's got women on his mind.

According to this scientist, even the slightest thought of an attractive girl—or the mere presence of particular female company—usually causes an obvious increase in beard growth.

Picture #17—"I Want You All to Myself"

In courting or flirting, one of the more interesting signs of Body Language occurs when the man and woman have progressed to the talking stage. It is at this time, in a social situation, that one (or both) of the parties becomes *possessive* and tries to keep any third person from intruding.

To do this, the man or woman usually assumes a protective stance, using his or her body—arms, shoulders, face—to shield the person he or she is talking to from others. If it is a man, for example, he may keep any third person from intruding by leaning one hand against the wall, facing the girl, with his back to the surrounding people. Or he may simply stand, with his arms folded, or hands on hips, shielding the girl with his entire body.

The man or woman using these Body Language signs is saying, in effect, *"I want you all to myself."* And to any third party who may be seeking to intrude, he or she is saying, *"Please go away. Leave us alone."*

Picture #18—"I Don't Want to Be Noticed"

For various reasons, certain people do not wish to be noticed, in a social situation. It may be that they have something to hide. They may feel unattractive or ashamed of their clothes or appearance as they compare themselves to others. They may feel they are too tall, or short, or fat, or ugly. They may feel they are not smart enough—or they may be embarrassed by their speech or lack of education. Whatever the reason, such people tend to stand shyly or bashfully on the sidelines. They try to remain quiet and unnoticed.

They may just sit and stare. Perhaps they will read a magazine or newspaper. A woman of this type might be the one who volunteers to set out the refreshments or wash the dishes, while all the others are eating, drinking, and enjoying themselves. A man of this type will probably stand, with his hands in his pockets, staring at the floor, eyes downcast, as in Picture #18.

Such people tend to do whatever will make them less noticed, or even unattractive. They tend to dress plainly, unobtrusively, as this picture shows. All their actions seem to spell out this message: *"Please don't notice me. If you do, I may make a fool of myself in some way. Just leave me alone. I'll be all right. Find someone else to talk to."*

Picture #19—The Sign of Silent Approval

One of the secrets of Body Language is the way it tells you when someone is silently agreeing with you. This phenomenon was discovered by Dr. Albert E. Scheflen, who noticed it in his studies of people speaking in small groups.

If you want to know when someone agrees with you—even if he or she says nothing—look at the way this person is standing (or sitting). Often you will find that his or her position is the same as yours.

In Body Language, this is a sign of approval or agreement. And when reinforced by other movements, such as a wink, a nod, or the pursing of the lips, it means more than just a simple, *"Yes, I understand you."* It signifies vigorous approval.

Here is a curious fact you can test. It has been noticed that when several people in a gathering agree with what one person is saying, if he shifts the position of his body, the others quickly do the same. Try it the next time you are chatting with a small group of people in your living room, or where you shop, or work, or play. As you speak, try to notice who among your friends is sitting or standing in the same position you are. Then try crossing your legs, or uncrossing them. Try folding your arms, or unfolding them. Try lighting a cigarette, and look around you to see if this prompts someone else to do the same. If you are standing, start motioning with your body toward some physical object, like a window, door, or corner of the room. Do this by moving toward it, gradually, without saying anything, and see if the others start moving with you. If you are all standing near some chairs, try sitting down, and see how many others do the same.

In this manner, it is possible for you to literally control the movement of other people's bodies, as a test to see whether they agree with you or approve of your point of view. When they follow your "silent commands" unconsciously, without realizing it, it is a sure sign, according to Dr. Scheflen, that you have made them think as you wish and that your thoughts are their own.

Picture #20—"Don't Bother Me. I Don't Want to Get Involved."

There are certain specific things that both men and women do with their bodies to indicate that they do not wish to be approached on a social level, in matters of love or friendship. At a party, or any social gathering, whenever you are thinking of introducing yourself to a stranger—or even if you wish to strike up a conversation with someone you know—you can often tell *beforehand* from observing these signs, whether you will be greeted with warmth and friendliness or whether you will be given the "cold shoulder."

Are the person's arms clasped defensively, as in Picture #20? Is the person's posture stiff, rigid, or tense? Is the person's face pinched and drawn? Does the person avert his or her eye when you try to catch it? Does this person turn away every time you look at him (or her)? Are the person's legs tightly crossed?

All of these are signs that the person does not wish to be approached—for whatever private reason he or she has. It is as if the person were saying, *"Don't bother me. I don't want to get involved. I am closed to any approach."*

Pictures #21-24—"I'm Interested in You."

At any party or social gathering, when two people are interested in getting to know each other better, they use Body Language to telegraph their availability. Will the other person be "cold" or friendly? The rule of thumb is that whatever actions are tense, tight, and reserved, mean *"Stop!"* or *"Proceed with caution."* And whatever actions are open, friendly, or relaxed, mean *"Go. Proceed with confidence. I like you. I'm interested in you. Let's get to know each other better."*

The eye is the all-important factor in making the first advance. It begins first with furtive glances as in Picture #21. If the other person is at all interested, he or she will return these glances. Then the glance is held a little longer than necessary—with perhaps a slight smile. If the other person is at all interested, he or she will respond in the exact same way.

Where two men or two women are concerned, both may walk toward each other, and either one may initiate the conversation. Where a man and a woman are involved, it is the man who is usually expected to make the first move (although it is permissible for a woman to do so).

To start the conversation, a question is first posed. And this may be on any topic—even a question you have been meaning to ask this person for a long time, provided it isn't too personal. It may be a question about clothing, cars, or jewelry, or a question pertaining to the social event itself, or some local bit of news. The possible interests of the other person must be taken into account, too.

The only difficulty that may arise is when the person you wish to strike up an acquaintance with sends both "Stop" and "Go" signals, with his or her body—a smile, perhaps, but tightly crossed arms; a friendly remark, perhaps, but a tendency to move away.

The one who is sending both "Stop" and "Go" signals may simply be having difficulty deciding whether you are the type of person he or she can get along with, whether your interests and abilities are similar, or whether he or she "measures up" to you (remember, a person can be ashamed of his or her appearance, speech, education—any number of things).

When this happens, you must counter each "Stop" sign with a "Go" sign of your own. For example, if the person's arms are closed tightly, you must make sure that your arms are open and relaxed. If the person's posture is rigid, try relaxing yours. If the other person is frowning, respond with a relaxed smile.

In courting or flirting, a man will typically stand or sit uncomfortably close to the woman he is interested in, as in Picture #22—without touching, which (since he is a stranger) is considered socially unacceptable.

The aggressively available woman will use many of the same techniques (sitting uncomfortably close to the man she is after, for example, taking advantage of his uneasiness as a means of throwing him off-balance). Unlike a man, however, it is considered socially acceptable for a woman to touch a man. She may touch his arm, for example, to ask if he has a match. She may steady his hand, if he offers to light her cigarette. She may touch his arm, his shoulder, his thigh, or hand while talking, as in Pictures #23 and #24.

LIVING PICTURES THAT REVEAL ALL

To understand Body Language is to realize that it is a step-by-step process, like the pictures on a strip of film.

Individually, it shows a frieze or still picture. But taken as a whole, an entire panorama of actions passes before your eyes— body motions with hidden meanings, a secret code that can be cracked.

Here are several examples that show what Body Language can reveal in ordinary, everyday life.

SEES WHAT NEIGHBOR IS DOING

Harriet D. used this method to detect the woman who was gossiping about her and spreading false rumors in the neighborhood. At a tea party which Harriet gave for several close friends, she used her "Mental Binoculars" to study each of the guests, and discovered one woman in particular—Mrs. G. F.—nervously fidgeting with her hands (see Pictures #5-6). Whenever Harriet spoke to her, she would sort of jump, and turn to look at her in a startled, wide-eyed way. She would glance nervously at the other guests, and then at Harriet, eyes narrowed, with the suspicion that maybe Harriet knew.

And at that moment, Harriet *did* know. She could sense the hatred, fear, and suspicion in this woman. As Harriet remarked: "I could actually *see* her with the next-door neighbor, gossiping over coffee, and saying all sorts of nasty things behind my back. I could just hear what they were saying, too. Vile things, nasty things. It was embarrassing to think that I had confided in her."

Mrs. G. F. hastily excused herself and left the party. And now that Harriet knew who it was (her friends confirmed her suspicions), she was able to defend her name and reputation.

SEES WHAT THIEF IS DOING

In the case mentioned earlier in this chapter, Harold J. discovered the culprit by standing up suddenly, and gazing menacingly around the room. Everyone was staring at him, except one individual, Norman E., who was sort of slouching in his seat, eyes downcast, staring at his desk.

Harold described what his "Mental Binoculars" had revealed, in sharp focus: "It wasn't hard to see what he (the thief) was doing. He was sneaking around my office, riffling through the papers on my desk, opening the drawers, and removing valuable stock certificates and other documents. These were all later found among his (the thief's) belongings."

SEES WHAT WOMAN IS DOING

In the case of Laura D., mentioned in the beginning of this chapter, here are the signals that both I and the man she was signaling to, Steve W., noticed:

"Whenever she looked at me—which was frequently—she sort of thrust her breasts forward," said Steve, "stood straighter, and would start preening. At these times, she stroked her hair . . . her thighs . . . or pushed her hair away from her face. Occasionally, she would sit down to check her makeup and would sweep her hand under her thighs to rearrange her dress. Lips pouting, she would stand and roll her hips from side to side or thrust them forward slightly, glancing furtively in my direction. When I approached, she would stand in a relaxed manner, arms out at her sides, in a kind of welcoming gesture."

A UNIVERSAL LANGUAGE

In the past few years, hundreds of researchers across the country have turned to the study of Body Language—among them, psychologist Paul Eckman, of the Langley Porter Neuro-psychiatric Institute, in San Francisco.

His theory—and I agree—is that if you understand Body Language (the unconscious movements we all make, to indicate what we feel), you can speak it. He says that certain clearly understood gestures of the face or body mean the same thing all over the world—a kind of "universal language" that enables you to "speak" to any foreigner, silently, without uttering a word of his language.

To prove this, he set out with half a dozen photographs—showing happy faces, sad faces, angry faces, surprised faces, disgusted faces, fearful faces—and he asked people in half a dozen different parts of the world to name the emotions portrayed in each photo. All over the world, he found, people correctly identified each photo. Other scientists caution, however, that it is a mistake to interpret single body movements alone.

All body signals must add up to a correct total if the meaning is to be accurate.

A NEW WAY OF LOOKING AT THINGS

It is hoped that you will see in these methods a new way of looking at things that can help you in your personal life. For example, say you have a troubled friend or neighbor. By looking at him in this new way, you will come to know the nature of his problems and be able to exercise sympathy and understanding. What might otherwise have appeared to be rudeness or thoughtlessness on his part, you will then understand to be a special problem he is trying to resolve.

These methods can help you understand a wife, a husband, a son or daughter better. They can help you strengthen and unite all family ties.

Psycho-Command Power #3

A SECRET LISTENING DEVICE
THAT LETS YOU HEAR
WHAT OTHERS ARE THINKING

In just a few moments, you are going to be able to *hear* the secret thoughts of others. Yes, you are going to be startled, amazed—but you are actually going to hear the secret thoughts of any person, and that is a solemn promise.

In fact, you will be able to hear these secret thoughts across a room, a city, or a continent— through actual physical barriers, such as walls, floors, ceilings, and doors.

How? Because I am also going to show you how to use a "secret listening device" that will enable you to hear what others are really saying—what they are really thinking—when they speak to you.

Why am I so certain of this? Why am I so sure this "secret listening device" will work for you—right now? *Because, when people talk, they reveal what they are secretly thinking,* even though they do not realize it.

Like a secret coded message—that becomes crystal clear when you lay a decoder over it, blocking out certain words—this method shows you what others are really saying. In a flash, the secret thoughts, hidden desires, strange motives, and plans of others are revealed—through actual words.

Suddenly the message is clear—the "smoke screen" of lies, fancy words, and double-talk disappears—and you know what others are really thinking.

HOW TO "TUNE" IN ON THE THOUGHTS OF OTHERS

In a sense, the power that you, and I, and everyone has to "read" between the lines of what others are saying, makes your *mind* a secret listening device (although I will show you how to use a real one, in just a little while). True, it is a "forgotten" power, in many cases, but one which you possess, all the same.

Psychologists have discovered that when people speak, they may not always mean what they say, *but what they're really thinking is often revealed in* the way *they say it.*

DISCOVER THE SECRET MOTIVES AND HIDDEN DESIRES OF OTHERS

Now, for the first time, you will see the secret motives and hidden desires of men and women you know! You will understand why they do the things they do and what they're likely to do next!

You'll discover the "dead giveaways," slips-of-the-tongue, and other important clues that tell you what others are thinking, as well as specific techniques for making them reveal themselves.

TO KNOW IS TO CONTROL

It's almost impossible to exaggerate the importance of being able to judge people accurately, to know what an individual is thinking or feeling in a given situation. When you know the other person's thoughts—

* You can pick the people who can help you reach your goals.

* You can avoid placing your trust in an unworthy person.

* You can spot the person who's out to trick you, financially or otherwise.

This chapter reveals methods you can use to perceive clearly what goes on inside an individual's mind—even when he's doing his best to play it deadpan or hide his (or her) intentions.

HOW TO HEAR THE SECRET THOUGHTS OF OTHERS

Next time you're holding a conversation with someone, look directly at him—actually meet his eyes and concentrate. Don't let your thoughts wander, *really listen to what he's saying and how he's saying it.*

Don't respond immediately when it's your turn to speak. Use silence as a device for discovering other people's secret thoughts. Silence has an amazing effect on people: it makes them reveal themselves.

Try this, the first chance you get. When you're in conversation with someone, don't rush in with something to say the moment he stops speaking. Let silence take over for a few moments. The other person will jump in to fill the silence, and almost invariably, he'll uncover himself, reveal thoughts, provide important clues.

SHE HEARS WHAT'S REALLY ON HIS MIND

Want to see how this "secret listening device" works in actual practice? Here's an example taken from a real-life situation.

Mr. J.: "I'm sorry I came home so late, honey. We had to work late at the office."

Mrs. J.: (silence).

Mr. J.: "Afterwards, I took this customer out to eat. We stopped at the Bowling Alley, played a couple of games, and then had supper."

Mrs. J.: (silence).

Mr. J.: "Well don't look at me like that. I called you. I told you not to wait up for me. The way you look you'd think I had a girlfriend at the office or something."

Mrs. J.: "Do you?"

Mr. J.: "Oh, look. Just because I drive the secretary home once in a while doesn't make me a criminal. What've you been doing, spying on me?"

Mrs. J.: (silence).

Mr. J.: "Okay, okay. So she went with us to the Bowling Alley. I told you. We all worked late. What're you trying to do? Make a Federal case out of it."

Mrs. J.: "No, dear. You are. Your secretary never even crossed my mind. But now that you mention it, just what *were* you doing!"

From this you can easily see the effectiveness of silence as a thought-revealing device. Try it on someone you know. Try it, for example, on your wife or husband some time. Just stop what you're doing, look at this person—and after a while, he or she will start talking, revealing hidden thoughts, plans, and desires.

To sharpen your skills, give it a couple of trials with friends or members of your family. Try it with neighbors, co-workers— even your boss. See how they start to reveal things that are really on their minds.

LISTENING BETWEEN THE LINES

A lot of times you can learn more by what the other person doesn't say than by what he does.

"Let's see how you're doing," the boss says. "Not too bad," he muses, as he stands over your shoulder. But you wonder, does the boss *really* think you're doing a satisfactory job? Or is he hiding disappointment?

At home, you try to get your neighbor interested in a money-making deal. Your neighbor says, "Let me think it over." You suspect he isn't the least bit interested. On the other hand, you think he might try to pull a fast one and try to sneak all the profits for himself. If only you knew . . .

Or perhaps your friend comes up to you and suggests a business deal. He looks sincere. He sounds sincere. Yet you're not sure you've got him sized up properly. If only you could be sure ..

> There is only one way you can be sure, and that
> is by listening between the lines. People don't al-
> ways put everything into words for you. Watch for
> the changing tone of voice, the expression on his
> face, his mannerisms, his gestures, the movements of
> his body.

Note the amount of strain he shows. Compare his behavior
in the present situation to his normal behavior. His expression,
his use of gestures, other physical signs give you your answer.

Is he weighing his words carefully? Do you sense a wariness
in the way he answers questions? *Why* is he wary? Why does he
hesitate before he speaks? Is he afraid that a slip of the tongue
may get him into trouble?

REVEALS HER HIDDEN THOUGHTS

Julie K. was an especially attractive young girl, who drew
sighs and glances from all the men. She could have all the dates
she wanted, Mike T. thought. That's why he was so surprised
when she responded with a "Yes" to his request to take her out.

Mike soon realized, however, that her intentions were not
what they seemed. Her secret thoughts, he soon discovered,
were that she was too good for him, that it was, in some way,
beneath her to show any interest in him at all. He perceived this
from her casual, offhand manner, her "coldness" and air of
snobbishness. Clearly, she had only accepted his invitation to
show herself off socially, and perhaps even out of spite, to get
back at someone she was really interested in.

Mike decided, then and there, never to let himself be "used"
by her in this manner again. He did not ask her for a second
date, and she was no doubt surprised that he had read her secret
thoughts.

HOW TO TURN UP THE "VOLUME"
OF YOUR SECRET LISTENING DEVICE

To find out more clearly what another person is thinking, it
is sometimes a good idea to interrupt him, and throw him an
unexpected question. His reaction, when you catch him off-

guard like this—the expression on his face, the ease and sincerity of his smile, the loudness or softness of his voice—can sometimes reveal, more clearly than words, what he is really thinking.

Does he immediately become defensive and argumentative? Does he stammer and start to act unsure of himself? Or does he continue easily, taking your question in stride?

For example, in the case of Mike T., just mentioned, to assure himself that he wasn't simply imagining things—that Julie was, indeed, acting too haughty, too "good" for him—he suddenly turned to her, on the way home from the theatre, and asked if she'd like to stop off at a diner for a hot dog. She had been expecting to be taken to a fancy restaurant, and she reacted with surprise and horror. "Certainly not!" she snapped at him, "You promised to take me to the Blue Swan, and that's where we're going."

USING YOUR SECRET LISTENING DEVICE
IN THE PRESENCE OF OTHERS

Your secret listening device may be used in the presence of others, without uttering a sound, to find out other people's moods. For example, when a person you know, who is usually carefree and converses with you easily, is suddenly withdrawn and distant, you know that something is wrong. Something has happened to make this person nervous, tense, or depressed. Therefore, you can *hear* it in his words, as well as his actions.

Is he (or she) talking more today about money than he usually does? Does this person seem overly concerned today about health matters? Is he complaining more than usual about wives, children, lenders, creditors, bills, cars, in-laws, or what have you? If so, he may be having real difficulties along these lines in his personal life.

It's because you have a clear picture of what's normal for certain people—friends, neighbors, co-workers, members of your family—that you can make this secret listening device work for you.

To turn up the "volume" of your secret listening device— and hear more clearly what's really on this person's mind—a direct question usually brings you the answer, with a good friend. You may simply ask, "Anything wrong?" or "You seem somewhat preoccupied this morning. Anything bothering you?"

In nine cases out of ten, they'll pour out their hidden thoughts to a ready, willing listener—*you*.

LISTENING DEVICE
REVEALS NEIGHBORS' PROBLEM

Willis D. and his wife, Betty, were neighbors of mine, who had come to be good friends over the years. I saw them every day, chatted frequently over the fence with them, and we would often exchange small favors. I knew that trouble was brewing, however, the morning I said hello to Willis, and he walked right by me.

The man was obviously troubled. The question was: About what? Finally, one day when I happened to be raking leaves, I saw Willis and his wife in the back yard, apparently relaxing.

"Hi!" I said. "What's got into you two lately? I haven't seen hide nor hair of you for days. One day last week, I said hello to Willis, and he walked right past me."

Well, that was all that was needed to break the ice. Willis and Betty came over to the fence, and apologized. "I'm sorry about that little incident," Willis said. "The fact is, we're just plain worried about my daughter."

"I don't like the boys that she's been going out with lately," Betty said.

"Neither do I," said Willis. "They're a bad lot. We've forbidden her to go out with them. But she sees them every day at school. She likes them, and I just don't know what we can do about it."

"I'm worried sick," Betty said. "You don't know what it is to have a daughter. I can just see her running off with every boy she meets, in cars, drive-ins, dark corners. Maybe it's just our imagination, but I can't eat, I can't sleep on account of it."

"And what will the neighbors think?" Willis added. "I can tell you. You're a good friend. But what about the others. It's so embarrassing. If it ever got out. . . ."

"Calm down, the both of you," I said. "Sandra's a good girl. I've watched her grow up, and I know. You're just worrying needlessly. She would never do anything to hurt you. You'll see I'm right."

As it turned out, I was right. And all it had taken was a simple question, on my part, to find out that there was really nothing wrong, and that my neighbors were still good friends, as well as neighbors.

SECRET LISTENING DEVICE REVEALS
THE TRUTH ABOUT OTHERS

To get along with others, you need the truth. Your logic, your reasoning, the soundness of your decisions, depend upon it. Without it, you're stymied. With it, you can use your judgement, your sense of fairness. One purpose that certainly must not be yours is that of the snooper, the person whose probing is motivated by morbid curiosity. The plain fact is, however, that in many situations in life you simply must have the truth, before you can exercise proper judgement.

One secret device for getting the truth from others is simply to tell them *why* it is essential for you to have the information. Bring home to the person who is reluctant to level with you exactly what's at stake. Be specific. Your reason may be anything from peace of mind to matters involving cash, a career, or an individual's safety.

DISCOVERS TRUTH WHEN CHILD
PERSISTENTLY LIES

Nona J. was at her wits' end when she tried to find the money she'd put aside to pay the rent—and it was gone. A frantic search through every corner of the house had turned up nothing. There was only one possibility left—a long shot, but still worth trying.

Nona's two children, Billy, age 5, and Nancy, age 4, were the only ones, besides their father, who could have taken it—and it certainly wasn't their father, since the money was still in the drawer when he left for work that morning.

The two tots were called into the living room, and there Nona sat them down and asked if they had seen the money. A look of surprise crossed the children's faces, they glanced at one another, and then Billy shook his head no. "We didn't see any money, mommy," he said. "Did we, Nancy?" Nancy shook her head no.

Nona leaned forward, gazing at them intently. "Think carefully, children. Are you *sure* you didn't see the money lying around?"

Billy glanced at Nancy again. Both children shook their heads no.

"Well, if mommy can't find the money," Nona said, "she won't be able to pay the rent. And do you know what that means?"

Again the children shook their heads no.

"It means we'll have to move out of the apartment. And we have nowhere to go. We'll have to move everything out on the street . . . the furniture, your clothes, your toys, your dolls . . . everything, out on the street. And we'll have to sit on the sidewalk, *all* winter long, and it'll be cold, and you'll be shivering . . .but that's where we'll have to stay, and you and mommy and daddy will have to sleep outside, in the cold, too. Are you *sure* you didn't see the money anywhere. Mommy won't hurt you."

"We-e-ll," Billy said, pausing for a moment, "it couldn't be the *play* money, could it?"

"Yes, the play money!" Nancy said.

Billy reached into his pocket and took out a roll of money, which he held out.

"Why, *yes*," said Nona, "*that's* it! Tell me, children, how did you find it?"

"Well," Billy said, "we saw this money on the dresser, and we wanted to use it—you know, to play store, and we thought it was play money."

"Yes," Nancy chimed in. "And I bought a hat, and a fur coat, and Billy bought a car, and some groceries. It was fun."

"But why didn't you tell mommy you took the money, Billy?" said his mother.

"We thought it was play money, mommy. And when you said it was *real* money, we were scared you would punish us."

"*Yeah*," said Nancy, "we were *scared*. But we don't want to live in the street," she whimpered. "Please don't let them put us in the street, mommy."

Nona hugged the children and assured them that everything would be all right now. And she told them how clever it was of them to see that it was actually real money, and that everything was fine now, because they were so grown up.

*   *   *   *   *   *

From this example, you can see that another secret device for getting the truth—in addition to telling *why* you need it—is to provide an incentive of some sort. Make it advantageous in some way for the other person to provide you with the information you need. In this case, it was the threat of being put out on the street. But it works with grownups just as well as it does with children. For who can refuse an honest plea for help in an emergency—who can deny a person the truth, when it is obvious his (or her) job, livelihood, or safety depend upon it. Very few, indeed.

Another secret device for getting the truth is to *minimize* the consequences. "If I tell, the kids will all be mad at me," the child says. "If I tell, I might get a lot of people into trouble," the grownup thinks. In this case, your answer should be, "I will explain it to them," or "I will see to it that nothing will happen," if you feel you can do this. If not, you may be able to point out that the consequences of *not* revealing the truth will be much worse. Or you may say, "Really now, don't you think you're exaggerating a little?" And point out how others will respect the person all the more for taking the difficult but honest path.

An *indirect* question is another good device: "Can you spell that out in more detail?" or "I'm not quite sure I understand." These will often get the person to elaborate in much greater detail what he said before.

Finally, a very powerful device for getting at the truth is to pretend you don't know certain facts, when, in reality, you do. This will often encourage the other person to make a slip-of-the-tongue, simply because—when he hears the facts all wrong—he will start to correct you. For example, say you suspect someone of taking a tool from your garage. You *know* that no one else had access to the garage, because no one else knew where the key was. Instead of saying this, however, you say:"I think I left my keys with your son before I went away." "No, no! You gave *me* the keys . . ." Now, of course, it is too late, and he is forced to continue his explanation.

If, of course, you know most of the facts, you have merely to reveal all that you know. This puts you in a strong position, and practically forces the other person to reveal the truth . . . drop all pretense and make a clean breast of it.

A final word of advice is to avoid all questions that can be answered with a simple "yes" or "no." A flat yes or no often leaves you flat, especially if the answer is untrue. And even if it were true, you'd need to ask so many "yes" or "no" questions to get full details, that the "machine gun" effect could easily make the person clam up or shy away from you. Instead, use the various methods revealed in this chapter to encourage the person to answer you fully, completely. When you do so, he will often reveal the truth—even against his will.

THE TELEPHONE AS A SECRET LISTENING DEVICE

Try these methods the next time you speak to someone on the telephone. With the first technique, for example, just pause, and wait for the other party to fill in the gap—and after a while, he or she will start talking, revealing hidden thoughts, plans, and desires.

Use it as a mood detector. Watch for a changing tone of voice. Is the person weighing his words carefully—hesitating, perhaps, to avoid a slip-of-the-tongue?

Turn up the "volume" by asking certain questions, revealed in this chapter. This will give you a clearer idea of what he's thinking. Listen for his reactions. Does your question throw him, or catch him off-guard? The loudness or softness of his voice can tell you a lot about how nervous or confident he is.

Use it as a truth-getting device, with the various steps just mentioned. The telephone is truly a miraculous listening device —that knows no barriers in distance or space—and can tell many tales beyond what the speaker intends.

Psycho-Command Power #4

HOW TO COMMAND RICHES
OUT OF THIN AIR!

Does this surprise you? Does it seem like a radical idea? I am going to prove to you that you *can* command riches to appear—seemingly out of thin air.

> The purpose of this chapter is to prove to you that the basic idea of "something out of nothing"—the power to cause mental images to take on the form and shape of the things you desire—is a reasonable, proven, scientifically valid, and attainable goal—although it may not seem so at first.

Instantly and automatically—as automatic as the reading of these pages—I am going to show you how to turn thought-forms into the shimmering gold of wealth, happiness, love fulfillment, and spiritual completion—by commanding them to appear, seemingly out of nothingness!

It will seem like a miracle. Not someone else's miracle, but **your** miracle. A miracle that you can see, feel, touch, and possess. You'll believe it and know it's true when you slide behind the wheel of that new car, sign the papers giving you possession of a lovely new home, or recline on the first-class deck of an ocean-going luxury cruiser. It will not be a dream. It will be a reality.

I am so sure this secret will work for you that right now I am going to ask you to decide what it is you want most. Vast fortunes have been built with this method. Every person who has acquired great wealth, power, happiness, and contentment, has used this secret.

Starting immediately, it can bring you money . . . a golden flow of riches, money in the bank, to purchase a new car, a new wardrobe, new furniture, a new home or apartment, beautiful new clothes or jewelry.

It can attract a romantic partner, for purposes of marriage. Or, if married, it can better your relationship with your mate. It can bring you friends, an interesting social life, and much more. It can bring you anything you desire!

All this is a proven fact—scientific in every way. It seems impossible, yet with a simple explanation, it becomes so clear that anyone can understand it—and even the most learned scholars, scientists, and die-hard skeptics readily agree that, yes—it *is* so, it *is* possible.

SOMETHING OUT OF NOTHING—
A REASONABLE EXPLANATION

Every object in existence first existed in someone's mind. Look around you, and you will see how true this is. A teacup, a pencil, an automobile, a zipper, a stocking, the clothes on your back—all existed first only as an idea in someone's mind.

You, yourself, are the result of this miraculous Law of Creation. Everything you have—and do—are the result of it. Your goals, your desires, the things you have now, first existed only as ideas in your mind.

No one has ever *seen* a thought except the thinker. Thoughts, ideas, mental images are **invisible to all** except the thinker himself. Some say thoughts *can* be projected to other people's minds. But this depends upon the *will* of the thinker.

And some say it is possible to receive others' thoughts—without their knowledge or consent. And so it may well be. Scientists even go so far as to say that thought vibrations can be registered by a machine and seen as squiggly lines on a graph. That may be true, but it's a far cry from actually seeing a thought. To all others—to most of us, in fact—thoughts are invisible. And *only our own thoughts* are seen by us.

The same is true of hearing impressions. It may be possible to project them—silently, without uttering a sound—and it may also be conceivable to hear other people's thoughts, if you know how. But to most of us—the vast majority of human beings—thought is a silent, invisible process, seen and heard only by the thinker.

WHY THE SEEMINGLY IMPOSSIBLE IS POSSIBLE

Each of us, therefore, lives in a vast invisible universe—silent and invisible to others, but clear as life and plain as day to us. *To each of us*, our minds are a kingdom, alive and filled with the splendor of our dreams, desires, and goals. We can see these goals clearly. Each of us can see and even hear the things he wants—within our minds.

Thoughts are *real*—thoughts are *things*—to the thinker. And each of us *knows* that *anything and every-thing* that we are capable of wanting and having in the inner world of our minds is possible in the outer world. How do we know?

We know this because we have seen it, time and again—right on down from the miracles of the Bible to the miracles of our own day. Man dreamed of ships that could fly—and found that this miracle is possible. Man dreamed of a way to carry the human voice around the world—and found that possible. He dreamed of a way to ride instead of walk—and lo, the miracle of the wheel. He dreamed of a miracle engine—with the power of a thousand horses—in a single box, and found that miracle was possible. He dreamed of soaring to the moon—and found the moon was his.

Likewise, the human mind can materialize thoughts as well as any duplicating machine that makes synthetic diamonds—and each man *knows* his dreams are possible. How does he know? He knows—like a baby chick knows how to walk, minutes after emerging from the shell—because that knowledge *was placed within him* before he was born (somewhat like the knowledge that there is an afterlife that each of us instinctively feels).

His common sense tells him, as well. Riches and abundance are part of nature. It has been estimated that from just two parent rabbits, 10,000,000,000 rabbits could come into existence. Nature is profligate in all that she does. And the same Power that created worlds and stars without number has created riches and happiness in abundance for you. Think about that.

PSYCHO-MOTION PICTURE #1—LOVE

Psycho-Command can make the man or woman of your dreams appear before you—actually materialize in your life! (See Chapters 1-2 and 5-8 for methods to use.)

> If miracles as big as these—the miracle of the
> Universe, the miracle of birth and creation, the
> miracles of the Bible, and our own modern mir-
> acles—are possible, certainly little miracles, like
> money, love, health, and happiness are possible. For
> what is $100,000 or even a $1 million, compared to
> the vast, eternal Cosmos.

All around you, others—no better, no smarter, no harder
working than you—have obtained the miracles they desired. It
happens every day. Every day sick people become healthy;
lonely people find love and happiness; and poor people become
rich. There are approximately 90,000 millionaires in the United
States right now—and 5,000 more each year.

Who is to say that you can't be one of them? Remember,
God is profligate in all that He does—He does everything in a big
way. Will He lavish His gifts upon you? The answer is YES!
Perhaps you do not believe this is possible. But I am going to
prove to you that it's true—and that the idea of riches out of
thin air can work for anyone, man or woman, old or young, rich
or poor. It can magically transform your life!

HOW OBJECTS APPEAR—
SEEMINGLY OUT OF THIN AIR

How to build—from nothingness—riches out of thin air?
That is the question. What are the components, the building
blocks, that will give you "good measure, pressed down, and
shaken together?" Once again, the answer is that they are
ideas—thoughts, mental images, goals.

"But," you say, "what has this to do with the house I
want—the brick, the beams, the piping. Surely you are not
suggesting that all these come out of thin air?" My answer is
that your *idea* of these things, as well as the necessary steps to
bring them into being (*an invisible, mental plan*) is just as much
a part of the house as the brick itself, for without a plan there
would be no house.

Remember—there is no such thing as a house, or a car, or a
television set in Nature. Nowhere are they born or grow, except
in the human mind.

Now you may say that no one has ever made a house out of nothingness. You may point out that a house never *extruded* from someone's mind—*like ectoplasm from a medium.*But that is exactly what I am saying!

Any house that exists—or ever will exist—came out of the idea of a house, somewhere, long ago, in someone's mind, just as the idea for a television set, or a car, or anything else. And since ideas are invisible—to everyone except the thinker—the idea of the house, and the house itself, was born out of nothingness, out of thin air.

 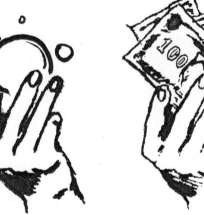

It's true! The amazing Miracle of Psycho-Command Power brings riches—seemingly out of thin air! Automatically makes things you desire appear in your life! Starting immediately—it can bring you money, love, power, friends, or anything else you want!

"But," you say, "learning the plan for obtaining a house is still not building it out of thin air; not the way the original builder—or anyone after him—makes a house, or car, or television set." *But that is exactly what I am claiming.*

Your idea is that it is possible to have it, and that you want it. Therefore, the idea of the house—and the house, itself—is yours, as much as anyone else's, since all things are possible. And as for the plan itself, *your* way of obtaining it may be different from the plan of the actual builder—*nevertheless, it* IS *a way of obtaining it.* It is your way of **bringing into existence something in your life which did not exist before.**

And the time, money, or anything else you spend in exchange for it—such as the time you are spending now, in exchange for the knowledge this book gives you—*makes* it

PSYCHO-MOTION PICTURE #2–JEWELS

With the money it brings, this method can materialize glittering jewels for you—seemingly out of nothingness! (For method to use, see Chapters 4-5 and also Chapter 9.)

yours, for it represents a piece of your life, your actual flesh and substance.

HOW ACTUAL CASH IN HAND APPEARS

That is why money is so valuable. The coins or paper are not valuable in themselves. It is what they represent—and they represent a slice in time of the actual life of the person who earned them.

> **You say you have no money? You are broke? That is why you are reading this book? To find out how you may obtain actual cash in hand? My answer is—right now—although you may not believe it, you can obtain any amount of money you desire— say, $35,000. How? By seizing hold of the idea of $35,000 in your mind and making it yours.**

The instant you decide that something—anything—is yours, it becomes yours in fact, as well as in the mind. That is why the religionists insist that we thank the Creator in advance for giving us what we ask for—even before we have received it.

INSTANTLY YOUR LIFE IS CHANGED!

The instant you envision something you desire, it takes form first as a tiny speck in the vast Cosmos of your mind.

If that is where you want it to stay—as a mental image or dream only—that is exactly where it remains. It may be that you doubt it is possible to receive the thing you wished for. Doubt effectively blocks all action, both mental and physical. Or it may be that you are afraid to see your desire blossom into physical reality. If so, it will remain an ever present, hovering dream, as long as you let it.

> **The instant you take mental possession of it, however—and decide firmly that it is yours, in both the inner and outer world—it begins to move toward you, or you toward it, looming ever larger and larger, until it is solid reality that you can see, feel, touch, and possess.**

What you can conceive—dream or imagine—mentally, you can receive. As long as you know what it is you desire, then by simply affirming that it is yours—firmly and positively, with no ifs, buts, or maybes—over and over again, from the minute you arise in the morning until the time you go to sleep at night, and as many times during the day as your work or activities permit, *you will be drawn* to those people, places, and events that will *bring your desires to you.*

THE SUPREME COMMAND FOR SUMMONING THE POWER THAT BRINGS RICHES OUT OF THIN AIR!

This method for obtaining riches—seemingly out of thin air—dates back to Biblical times. This secret has been found in the sacred scrolls of the Dead Sea, the Excavations of the Gobi Desert, and in the sacred monasteries of Tibet. Deep in the interior of the vast pyramid of Gizeh, in the King's Chamber, it has been found—each time "for the first time"! Yet its "newness" never fails to impress each new generation. *It must work for you, because it has worked for thousands of others, no better, no smarter, no luckier or harder working than you; it works every time!*

It is the very Law of Creation—and the basis of the belief in a Master Mind that created us all! In calling upon this power, I believe that we are really calling upon the Master Mind of the Universe. If you recollect the Bible, you will recall these words: "Created He him in His own image." I believe that all our minds are really the Master's Mind in miniature—that each of us actually carries a small part of God around with us, all the time, that permits us to communicate with Him.

This part of God, this mind, is like a **Speed-O-Matic Thought Duplicator**, an **Automatic Miracle Maker**—a **Psychic Transformer** capable of very real and supernatural powers—a **Pocket Insta-Commander** (with actual Cosmic batteries—see Chapter 8). And the secrets that make it work—like Insta-Buttons—are all over this book.

To claim that which you desire—to set this method into motion—*to start the materialization process*, here is a method which I call THE SUPREME COMMAND. It is an ancient ritual for calling on The Supreme Power that is guaranteed to bring about any event or condition you desire. If it is humanly possible, it is a certainty with The Supreme Command.

To begin with, set aside a quiet place where you will not be disturbed—and take a few moments to meditate on the truths that have been revealed thus far. When you feel that you are ready, and it is time, begin the following invocation ritual:

> I believe in myself and the Higher Power that resides both in my mind and in the mind of the Eternal One above. I call upon the Eternal One to enter these proceedings—for we are One, One Power, One Universal Energy, I a channel through which this Power can flow. I believe in this Power—united through me—that guides all our lives. What man has done, I can do with the Eternal One working through me because I believe 'If thou canst believe, all things are possible.' My greatest desire at this time is (the name of the event or situation desired). And to bring this situation about—*I can, I will, it is done* through the Universal Energy running through me.

Read these words carefully. It is not necessary to memorize them—but read them through and think about them. They are not ordinary words, but special words that are alive with power. And as you read them, they will feed themselves into your mind automatically. For this to happen, read them through several times. After that, sit back and relax.

Once inside your mind, THE SUPREME COMMAND goes to work at once . . . like a powerful undercurrent beneath the surface of the sea. Quietly it works, to transform your desire into its material duplicate. THE SUPREME COMMAND is faith and confidence in this Higher Power. And any expression of it, such as, "*I can . . . I will . . . It's been done before, and I can do it. I know I can . . .*" is THE SUPREME COMMAND that will bring this message across to the Higher Power that resides with you.

It is the *same* power that causes "instant healings" at revival meetings . . . It is the very power behind the marvel of Speed Hypnosis, discussed in Chapter 1. It has been used (in whole or in part) by every person who has ever acquired great wealth, power, or anything else! Without it, not a single miracle—out of the thousands of miracles we enjoy every day—money, love, friendship, cars, houses, TV—would be possible. For in every case, someone, somewhere, some time, had to believe these things were possible for them to happen.

Your desires are the individual powers or Psycho-Commands revealed in each chapter of this book—magic words, words of power, instructions that will help you achieve your desired goals. But the "key"—the "Open Sesame"—that absolutely guarantees your success—transforms your desires into reality—is the great "I CAN" that breathes life into your goals. Remember the wise old saying: "What you believe, you can receive."

YOUR GUARANTEE THAT THIS METHOD
WILL WORK FOR YOU

Do not doubt for one moment that you can command riches to appear in your life. Psycho-Command has worked for others, and it will work for you, too. **I know this to be true, from my own personal experience.**

For years I thought that riches were beyond my reach. No one knew the overwhelming despair of poverty better than this writer. A rat-infested tenement, with roaches and vermin, chipped and crumbling walls and ceilings, with water dripping through cracks and light fixtures, and no heat in the winter—these were my childhood experiences. Sleeping on the kitchen floor, to get some warmth from the gas stove; a whole family sleeping in one room in the broiling summer months. This was the way I lived for years.

Yet once I discovered this method, there followed the most remarkable years of prosperity I have ever experienced. Everything I asked for I received.

RECEIVES NEW CAR

One day, my mother told me that it was her dream that I should have a new car of my own. She described it as a large, golden limousine, with air conditioning, power steering, and much more. It seemed so far-fetched that I dismissed it as a dream. I felt that someday, maybe, in the distant future—but now? No. She told me this was the wrong way to think, and that she, herself, had made this mistake for years and years. But now all that was past. Very soon, she said, I would be receiving this new car—without any help, except the power of this method.

A strange sequence of events followed, so rapidly that even I am at a loss to explain exactly what happened. I found myself being lifted, from a low-paying job to a higher one—without any special knowledge or training, and so poor an education that I was embarrassed by it. And yet—to my surprise—my savings began to grow so rapidly, that within a very short time, I had accumulated enough money to purchase a new car.

Suddenly, I found myself staring at it, in an auto dealer's showroom. There it stood, big as life and plain as day! It was exactly as my mother had described it, in every detail. I touched it. I ran my hand over the smooth fenders. I felt numb—and a little dizzy—with the wonder of it. It was mine, all mine!

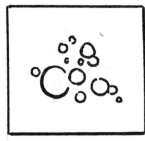 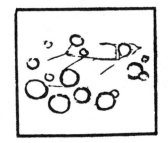 

PSYCHO-MOTION PICTURE #3—A NEW CAR

This method can make a new car appear in your   life! (For method to use, see Chapters 4-5.)

RECEIVES DREAM HOME

All my life, I wanted a home of my own. This seemed to me the most impossible dream of all. From the chipped and peeling windows of the tenement where I lived, all I could see were dingy, depressing buildings, each a crumbling monument of decay, with the people in them rotting as well.

And yet I knew that at the same time, other people—who had never known a minute of neediness—were living in beautiful homes in lovely neighborhoods, all over the country. Their children had rooms of their own—and here I was, a grown man, sharing a closet with three other people. It made me angry. It made me furious. I wanted a home so badly I could practically touch it. And in my dreams I could see it . . . would actually be living there. Then I'd awaken each morning to realize that I was still in a tumbledown apartment, with paint peeling from the ceiling.

But now the spell of this method was operating. I knew that very soon now the home of my dreams would emerge just as the automobile had. How or where, I did not know. I used the car to ride out into the country, looking. I searched for what seemed an eternity—although it was actually only a short time after I began to use this method.

Suddenly, there it was! A long, low, rambling ranch house, nestled in an immaculate suburban neighborhood. It had—not one, not two, not three—*11 rooms*; three bathrooms, four bedrooms, a living room, a dining room, a kitchen, a TV room, and a finished basement, with a garage.

The money had been accumulating all this time with this method. I had enough for a big down payment—and I bought the house, right then and there.

I stood there in helpless amazement. What had seemed impossible only a short while ago, had actually happened.

RECEIVES $20,000 CASH

There was one problem, however. The house was empty. And the small amount of broken-down furniture we had from our tiny apartment would never fill it. I had spent all the money I saved, and the prospects of getting more looked bleak indeed.

In addition, there were repairs to be made. The roof leaked, the boiler was in bad shape, some of the windows were warped and didn't shut right. The house needed painting and plumbing work.

I set this method in motion again—hoping against hope that it would bring the needed supply. As it turned out, my worries were needless, because it had never really stopped working. Within two years, this method brought me $20,000 in cash—seemingly out of thin air!

And to watch the house take shape, with complete carpeting, a new kitchen, new furniture—two sofas, nine chairs, four tables, and more—a dishwasher, a refrigerator, a washer and drier, a new sidewalk, two new driveways—was like looking at a movie, a Psycho-Motion Picture, with all these things popping into place, seemingly out of thin air!

I had walked out of that drab apartment—never to return again—and into a dazzling new life, filled to the brim with riches and luxuries I had never dreamed possible.

THERE'S A MIRACLE WAITING FOR YOU

Having proven to you riches can appear, seemingly out of thin air, I am now prepared to show you the continuation of this actual method for obtaining them. I call it my 5-Minute-a-Day Master Plan—an actual, step-by-step, money-making plan. *To make this method work for you,* you must decide if this idea—the idea of money—is what you want.

If this is what you want, and it is more important to you at the present time than anything else, you must firmly decide that it is yours. Say so, over and over again, and the plan will carry you, irresistibly and unrelentingly—all the way from your desire, to the formation of that desire *out of nothingness,* into a solid, tangible fact.

It is the same with love, friendship, or anything else. Do not worry about how these things will come to you. After you have set the process in motion *mentally* with this method, they will come. And all you need do, in effect, is wait for the desired results.

I don't care how skeptical you are now. This book will convince you. I don't care how lonely or sick at heart you feel right now. By the time you finish this book, you are going to be a new person. And you are going to have a new life! The problems you have now will vanish—and in their place will rush every good thing you've ever wanted!

Your circumstances will change from want to fulfillment, again and again, with each tick of the clock, and as you see these things actually happening in your life, you will come to know—as you have never known before—that everything the Master Mind has or is able to give, whether it be health, wealth, love, guidance, or protection, is yours!

In this book are true examples of how scores of people asked for—and received—life's blessings. I believe that, in making these requests, every one of them was invoking the Power of the Master Mind, the All-Wise, the Grand High Spiritual Leader of us all—the Hidden Power of the Universe!

Psycho-Command Power #5

YOUR INSTANT
FORTUNE MAKER!

The secret in these pages can bring you anything you desire! Anything! Easily and automatically! What is it you desire most?

Money? A new house? A luxurious apartment? A swimming pool or country club membership? A new car, perhaps? Or a new wardrobe? Money for entertainment? Or to educate your children? Or to pay off bills? To bring you peace of mind... How about a guaranteed automatic income for life, without work— of say, $5,000, $10,000, $15,000, $30,000, $100,000 a year or more?

What about love? Do you feel that life has cheated you of the love to which you are entitled? Do you feel lonely and unwanted? Does it seem that life has cast you aside—that there is no place for you, even though there seems to be a place for others, no better, no smarter than you? Is there someone you wish to attract? Someone you are ashamed or afraid to approach—*who you wish would come to you?*

The secret in these pages can bring you all these things and more—starting immediately! It is a secret which others are using right now! Many claim it has made their lives a heaven on earth—bringing wealth, love, and power to them, just like Aladdin's magic lamp!

Here is how Psycho-Motion Pictures—the science of *"living pictures"*—can bring about any event or condition you desire.*

HOW TO USE PSYCHO-MOTION PICTURES

How would you like to see a Psycho-Motion Picture right in your own living room, that would turn your desires into reality? Really, actually see this psychic movie come alive—to bring you anything you desire?

If seeing is believing, how would you like to watch your fortune—in dollars and ready cash—suddenly pile up right before your very eyes? Materialize into solid reality for you to see, feel, touch, and possess? Or see the man or woman of your dreams appear—seemingly out of thin air—and walk into your life?

If you wanted money, love, new friends, secret knowledge, a spiritual healing, or power over others, you'd simply play a psychic movie and watch the movie transform itself into solid reality—the future of your choice—right before your very eyes, with this method!

I am now going to show you a Psycho-Motion Picture (also called a **Cyclotron**)—several, in fact—*actual motion pictures in a book*! Then I am going to show you how to use these Psycho-Motion Pictures in your quest for the things you desire.

MOVIES THAT COME TO LIFE
TO BRING YOU ANYTHING YOU DESIRE

To "play" this new kind of movie, right now, and view it in your own living room, without any special equipment of any kind except this book—which is for you an "instant" Fortune-Maker, a Speed-O-Matic Desire Bringer, an Automatic Genius Maker, or Automatic Materializer—proceed as follows:

---

*I call this method **Cyclotronics**, for it is exactly like using an atom smasher—or cyclotron—that reassembles the invisible particles of space into a desired form. A Cyclotron is a *plan*.

On page 107, Psycho-Motion Picture #4—Money, you will find five rows of pictures—with four pictures across (from left to right) in every line. To view this Psycho-Motion Picture, simply look at each picture, from left to right, on the first line of pictures, just as though you were reading a book. Only in this case, instead of words, you will be "reading" pictures. Let your eyes stop, for a second, on each picture, then jump to the next—until you reach the end of the line. Then proceed to the next, from left to right, stopping at each picture—and so on, until you reach the bottom of the page.

And, lo and behold, you will find that these pictures seem to move! Like an actual motion picture!

Now you *know* that the pictures are not really moving. Each is a separate picture, of something happening, or someone doing something. Each picture shows one thing, and nothing else. And yet, when viewed in the correct sequence, one-by-one, they all add up to something very definitely happening.

HOW PSYCHO-MOTION PICTURES WORK

Psycho-Motion Pictures are based on the scientific fact that for every action there is a *reaction*. Something will happen as a result of anything you do. Even if you do nothing, the principle of Psycho-Motion Pictures will work for you—because to do nothing is *still* doing something.

Here is how Psycho-Motion Pictures work: Every goal consists of several steps, each step like the picture on a strip of film. Once these steps are clearly framed in your mind—like pictures—it is but a simple matter to follow them. For they are like a plan, a Master Plan, that carries you easily along to your desired goal. Without a plan, you are like a cork, bobbing along, drifting aimlessly in the sea of life. Without a plan, you are a helpless victim, literally being pushed around by invisible forces, the tide of fortune, or *other* people's plans.

Psycho-Motion Pictures, on the other hand, can give new meaning, new direction to your life. They are like power steering, in that they can literally push you ahead to success with little or no effort—carry you irresistibly, unrelentingly along to your desired goal.

All successful people use Psycho-Motion Pictures, although they may call them by different names, such as mental pictures, images, or ideas. I prefer to call them Psycho-Motion Pictures, mental or psychic movies, because to me a plan is like a living picture—a picture of what I want and the steps necessary to get it—that comes alive in my mind, urging me toward that goal.

These steps, or successive stages of your plan, do not *have* to be pictures. They can be words or a list of words, like a checklist of things to do—magic words that set up powerful thought currents within your mind—that extend all the way from a conceived notion, to the formation of that idea—out of nothingness—into a solid, tangible fact.

Everything in life is a progression of steps. A baby must learn to crawl before it can walk. And when it learns to walk, it gets to its destination—not by gliding through the air—but step-by-step. It's the same with driving a car, eating—or making money.

Too many people, in fact 99 per cent, fail simply because they jump the gun. They want to skip from the first to the last steps—or perhaps they forget, or simply don't know what steps to take. They lash out in 50 different directions in the course of a lifetime, trying first this—and then that—failing at each, and calling it bad luck. They wander and drift aimlessly, wondering why success has eluded them.

But with a definite, step-by-step plan—ah, what a difference it makes! You cannot fail, because each step carries you along to the next, like a track for a Happiness Express. You may stall somewhere once or twice along the line, but you learn from your mistakes—so that you cannot fail again—your plan takes on a new direction, the right direction, with *one goal*. And because you have a plan, you must succeed.

PSYCHO-MOTION PICTURE—MONEY

That is what this Psycho-Motion Picture shows. It shows money, piling up, right before your very eyes. Not all at once—but rather step-by-step, like savings in a bank account. But does it stop? No, it continues! Your money earns money—

without your lifting a finger—it earns interest, or dividends, depending upon where you put it, in savings, stocks, or bonds.

When an opportunity is presented to you to make money, do you quit your job and take all of your savings and dump them blindly into some new-fangled scheme? No, of course not! You investigate the matter thoroughly, read books like this one, talk to people who know something about finance, find out everything you can about the money-making opportunity—and then, if it still seems profitable, if it seems like something you can do, you make your plan. That is what the second row of pictures shows.

You start your business at home, in your spare time—perhaps even on your kitchen table—without great risk or expense, at hours that suit you, without sacrificing evenings of fun with family or friends (see third row of pictures). Just an hour or two, a few nights a week, may be all you need to get started.

Do you need money to get started? If so, instead of spending a penny of your own, you do what all great fortune builders do. You go to any bank or reputable lending institution and borrow the money you need. You go in, sit down, explain your plan to the lending officer, and fill out the application. **Your loan will be approved, if you have followed this plan.** You use this money to start your business—at home, in your spare time—paying back your loan from the profits of your business (see fourth row of pictures).

Now, with a new and profitable second-income fortune coming in, your savings start to increase faster and faster, much faster than they did before. You may double your money and keep doubling it, over and over again. This money earns more money for you—like a giant "Money Magnet"—to double, triple, and quadruple your income. That is what the last row of pictures shows.

If you follow this simple plan, keep it always in mind, it will carry you irresistibly, unrelentingly along toward your fortune.

YOU CAN GET RICH QUICKLY AND EASILY

Yes, you *can* get rich quickly—with a plan—and planning is the basic, fundamental secret of Psycho-Command.

Right at this very moment, you hold in your hands the clearest road map to riches that is available today. Follow it step-by-step, and you're certain to hit the big money quickly and surely.

Once your income begins to pile up, you can have your own home, a big car, a cabin cruiser, charge accounts at the best stores. As your income increases you can gradually change to more expensive things, if you wish. Thus, you can shift from a low-priced car to an expensive luxury car, if you wish.

*Have confidence. You can—and will—*build a fortune with the secrets in these pages. We're ready now to explore the many ways in which you can make a fortune—all stemming from a basic plan. I'm sure that among the many ways of building a fortune which you'll learn in these pages, there is one way ideally suited to you. So let's get started, here and now.

YOU NEEDN'T STEP OUTSIDE
YOUR OWN HOME

Resolve, here and now, that you will build a big income at home, in your spare time. Why? Because a home business is probably the safest way you can start earning big money. There are very few home businesses that fail, because you don't depend on your home business to live. You still have your regular job. You are not paying extra money to rent a store, a factory, or office. You are the landlord for your spare-time business activity, which you can carry on in your basement, attic, backyard, garage, kitchen, living room, bedroom, den, spare room, or corner—even your pocket. And you can start it with little or no cash.

START WITH LITTLE
OR NO CASH!

Many beginning wealth builders think that they must invest several thousand dollars to start their business. Nothing could be further from the truth! I can show you hundreds of home-business operators earning $10,000, $20,000, $30,000 or more—in their spare time—who have hardly any money invested in their business.

You earn *more* in your own business, because all the profit is yours—you don't have to deduct the cost of big offices, high salaries, extra rent, light and heat costs, before you get your profit.

FOCUS YOUR MAGIC CAMERA—
YOUR DREAM MAGNIFIER

The first step, as was mentioned before, is to use your mind like a psychic camera, whose magic photo-lens—like a magnifying glass—brings your goal into clear focus and photographs it mentally or psychically, so that you know exactly where you are headed. Once this happens, your goal or desire begins to form in the real world, for you to see, feel, touch, and possess.

Without a goal, you are lost. You flounder from one paycheck to the next. But this one step—choosing a goal and sticking to it—changes everything.

DECIDE WHAT YOU LIKE BEST

To focus clearly on your goal, decide what you like to do best. Everybody has some hidden talent or desire, something they like to do—such as a hobby or a pastime—that they find themselves doing again and again, to relax, that makes them happy.

It can be sewing, or fishing, or reading—or even just watching television. If you like to watch television a lot, it means you have a good imagination—flair for creativity. As a television watcher, you undoubtedly know what pleases you, as well as what you don't like, or think can be done better. And because of this, you might have a hidden talent for writing, singing, entertaining, or photography, that you hadn't even suspected.

You say you like to watch television, but you don't think you'd like to do any of the things I've mentioned? And you still have no idea of what you think you might be good at? Very well, let me answer that by pointing out the fact that *what* you watch can be a clear indication of hidden desires, things you would like to do, or be involved in, that would make you happy.

Take the large number of games—for adults, as well as children—that are being advertised on television these days, and the many game shows aired on TV. Obviously, there must be a heavy demand for such leisure-time activities; otherwise, why would the advertisers spend all that money on commercials and game programs?

So, if you enjoy games—and think you can come up with a good one yourself—why not try your hand at it? All you need is a pencil and some paper, to write down your ideas. A trip to the local toy store, or game department of any shopping center, will show you the kind of games people buy—as well as the names of the many toy companies (printed on the boxes) where you can send your ideas. For more information on how to first protect your ideas with a patent or copyright—write to the Superintendent of Documents, Washington, D.C., for free details.

In their book, *21 Sure-Fire Ways to as Much as Double Your Income in One Year,** Jean and Cle Kinney tell of a man who does exactly this. He sells his toy ideas to toy makers for a percentage of the profits. His toy ideas chalk up annual sales of over $1 million, representing more than $50,000 in royalties to Marvin G.—all from a business that costs him absolutely nothing, except some time and imagination.

Do the cultural programs on television interest you? Even if you don't know a thing about dancing, you can start a dancing or ballet school, right in your own home, in your spare time, with this method. Simply take out a small $5 classified ad in your local paper, advertising this service. When enough "clients" call for appointments, for themselves or their children, take out another small ad, in the Help Wanted section, for an instructor— or ask a friend or neighbor if he or she would like to help you. When your ad starts bringing in customers, you can charge $5, $10, $15, or any amount you want for lessons.

The profit is all yours, if you do the teaching yourself. If you employ others to do it for you, you share the profits with

---

*Jean and Cle Kinney, *21 Sure-Fire Ways to as Much as Double Your Income in One Year* (West Nyack, N.Y.: Parker Publishing Co., Inc., 1970).

them. In fact, you can expand the operation into a regular music school, with your own instructors working for you and your clients paying for their own instruments (which you buy for them, and sell or rent to them at a profit).

I know one woman, Martha T., who started this way, and now has her own dance studio—an Academy of Dance, she calls it—right in her own home, and who regularly takes in $200 to $300 a week this way, averaging $15,000 a year, without lifting a finger!

Another spare-time wealth builder, Martin B., started a complete music school with this method and makes $30,000 to $35,000 a year from it. Yet he doesn't even know how to play an instrument!

Or perhaps you like sports. You don't have to be an athlete—or even know anything about sports—to make good money in this field. You can start a miniature golf course (I almost wrote "goldmine," because that's what it is) right in your own backyard. Even if you don't know a thing about golf, you can advertise this service in your local papers, with just a small $5 classified ad—and get a few friends together, who *do* know something about golf, to help you set it up, acting as "instructors" in *their* spare time. Then you get a piece of the profits, for your small efforts and the use of your property. Here is a business that practically runs itself, bringing you a second income without work!

You can charge $15 or $20 for lessons—and take half for yourself! You can rent a few golf clubs and other equipment from a nearby sporting goods store—only as you need it—and turn right around and rent the use of this equipment to your customers, for what it cost you, plus a small additional profit. You can branch out, and even sell golfing equipment to customers who want to buy it.

So you see, you actually *can* make money, simply by watching television—by using TV as the source for your Psycho-Motion Pictures—letting it give you money-making ideas.

Do the cosmetics commercials fascinate you? Why not become a home representative for one of the big cosmetics companies, like Avon, in your spare time. In his book, *The Fran-*

chise Boom,* Harry Kursh tells you all about this business, which enables you to work a few hours a day or just a few hours a week. Under this system, you start selling cosmetics at home, usually by demonstration through appointments. Lee W., mother of three, used this method—working about an hour a day—to earn about $150 a month. Today, she has a business of her own, supervising 120 employees, and making $40,000 a year!

START NOW

Beginning immediately, decide on the things you like to do best, for these are the things that will be easiest for you. Do you enjoy meeting people and having lively conversations? If so, selling may be your game. Here's an example of how selling, in your own home business, can pay off big . . .

RECEIVES $500 A WEEK!

Stewart R. was working on an assembly line. "At the factory," he says, "I looked around at all the men working with me, and I thought to myself, 'Is this me, in 25 years? Is this as far as I go?' "

In a matter of minutes, Stewart started his wealth flow, by deciding to use the same basic method just mentioned—becoming a home representative for a big company. He went into the cookingware business, selling Tupperware, with his wife, Mary.

Together, they quickly started grossing around $500 a week in this spare-time business. They couldn't get over it. Soon Stewart and Mary were in their new business full time, receiving five times as much—almost overnight!

THEY GET AN AIR-CONDITIONED CADILLAC!

Harry E. was a postal clerk in Phoenix, Arizona, supporting a wife and two children, paying off a mortgage, and meeting car

---

*Harry Kursh, *The Franchise Boom* (West Nyack, N.Y.: Parker Publishing Co., Inc., 1968).

payments each month—all on a salary of $80 a week. His wife, Edna, soon went to work as a part-time dealer for this same cookingware company, arranging the famous "house parties" for which this brand is known.

Edna did so well that her husband quit his job immediately and joined her full time. Almost overnight, Harry and Edna were living in a new home and driving around in a new air-conditioned Cadillac!

*   *   *   *   *   *

On the other hand, selling may not be your cup of tea. You may be awkward with words but very good with your hands! Do you like to make things, build things? Perhaps you like to fix automobiles, or home appliances, or television sets? If so, a spare-time service business may be just the thing for you. Or perhaps you have a green thumb—you like gardening? A nursery, greenhouse, or floral catering service—which you can start in your own home—may be the magic money-making shortcut that will bring you wealth!

YOU NEED NO SPECIAL ABILITIES

You need no special abilities or higher education to make this method work for you. You needn't be a college graduate— even a high school diploma is not necessary. Many of the wealthiest, most successful people today—people you see driving around in limousines and living in luxurious homes—have made it big without a single day of higher education.

All you need is the desire—a *strong* desire—to make money. Every man and woman who has accumulated a fortune had a "money dream" that motivated him. This "money dream" kept him or her alert, ready to trap a new idea, method, or process that could be turned into wealth. To make money, you must think about money—constantly!

MAKE PSYCHO-MOTION PICTURES
WORK FOR YOU

When you have decided on the various activities that inter-est you most—whether sewing, arts and crafts, swimming, mechanics, raising pets, or anything else—take a pencil and paper and make a list of them.

Once you have your list, examine it carefully. These are the things you enjoy doing best or that interest you most. Now, next to each one, try writing all the ways you can think of to make money, using this particular item. Next to sewing, for example, if this is on your list, you might put: arts and crafts shop, sewing school, dress-making service, quilts, draperies. Next to an item like swimming, you might put: health club, massage and physical fitness center, teaching, writing.

If mechanics is on your list, next to it you might put: fix and sell old cars, specialize in antique cars, open up a garage, sell new cars or racing cars, organize club for stock car racing, write articles about cars, take pictures of unusual cars and sell them to newspapers and magazines.

If raising pets is on your list, you might write: poodle grooming service, a kennel to care for pets while owners are away, a pet training service, a dog-walking service . . . and so on.

Your list can go on like this for several items, or just two or three. Now, examine this list again, and check off or circle only those items that meet all of the following requirements with a "Yes."

* Is it simple to run?
* Can it be run with little or no cash, or on borrowed money?
* Can it be run in my spare time?
* Can it be run without a large stock of items?
* Can it be run without a lot of help—preferably by one person or perhaps one or two helpers?
* Can it be operated in my home, on my property, or in a small rented space?
* Will it yield an immediate cash income?
* Can it grow quickly?

If the answer to all these questions is "Yes" (and in this book, all the businesses I recommend meet these requirements), then it is safe for you to begin. Here is a list of businesses—any one of which you may wish to begin—that pay big profits:

hauling service, wake-up telephone service, floral arrangements, home clothing store, day nursery, portrait studio, jewelry sales, dancing school, take-out food shop, drapery studio, auto driving school, Karate school, duplicate key stand, canoe rentals, coffee house, home paperback bookshop, bridge lessons, art gallery, music school, rooming house, boarding house, rubbish service, sandwich route, tourist rooms, home bakery, astrologer, massage studio, bicycle shop, model agency, boarding kennel, handbill distribution, carpentry, seashell jewelry, bookkeeping service, flower stand, carpet and rug cleaning, advertising specialties, miniature golf, golf instruction (indoors or outdoors), TV repair, escort service, hamburger shop, real estate agency, house painting, antique shop, household machine rentals, floor machine rentals, home greeting card shop, home typing service, remail service, foreign language school, hair stylist, diaper service, secretarial school, garment repair and alterations, sewing school, sound truck, hobby school, taxi service, limousine service, sports equipment, handbag design and repair, landscaping service, lawn spraying, car washing, locksmith service for homes and businesses.

WHAT HAS WORKED FOR SO MANY OTHERS MUST WORK FOR YOU

There are thousands of ways for you to become rich. Some ways will bring you money faster than others—some will start to bring you money immediately—and some require less time and energy than others.* What we want to do, here and now, is to help you pick a path to riches that will make you wealthy as quickly as possible.

With luck, you can make a fortune almost overnight. Then you can sit back and enjoy your new-found wealth or continue building greater wealth. Results may come instantly, or after a few days or weeks of accumulated effect. But results will definitely come—this I promise you—in the direction of your desired goal.

---

*All can be automatic if you hire others to do the work for you.

Whether you're a man or woman, old, young, married, unmarried . . . even if you haven't got a job . . . or are a member of a minority group . . . or have no permanent residence . . . this method can work for you!

One of the happiest days of your life will be the day you begin to receive a steady stream of dollars into your home. This money can soon flow into your home in a "5-foot high river of money," as one delighted home fortune builder remarked.

So look at the record. On nearly every page of this chapter, you'll learn about people just like yourself who hit it big in their own home business. If they can do it, so can you.

RECEIVES $20,000 A YEAR!

Albert R. began collecting "finder's" commissions for locating spare parts and used parts for auto repair shops in his vicinity. Working only afternoons and Saturdays, he was drawing $50 a week in his spare time. Then he gave it his full attention—and immediately began receiving more money, a steady stream of money—over $20,000 after taxes the first year alone!

RECEIVES $3,200 QUICKLY!

Here's a case that shows the value of "money consciousness"—how merely thinking about money keeps you alert, ready to trap a new idea that can be turned into wealth.

Eddie E., an $80-a-week repair man, had put $100 down on a new home, when he noticed—accidentally—that one of his new neighbors had, for some reason, sold his home without moving in. After looking into the matter, he found that any homeowner could sell before moving in, if he so desired. (The same is true for co-op apartments.)

Eddie put his house up for sale, and found that he could sell it immediately for $3,200 profit! After that, Eddie decided to try this again. He'd buy a home, by putting a small down-payment on it with his modest savings—sometimes living in it for a couple of months—and then sell it, for a profit. Today

Eddie is a wealthy man. And yet his money comes to him, literally, without lifting a finger!

RECEIVES $2,000 A MONTH!

William L. decided to try this method when he was only 18 years old! By the time he was 28, he was making $2,000 a month! Today—instead of houses—he sells jet planes. Every time he uses this method, he makes a half-million dollars. He figures he's so wealthy he "could spend $1,000 a day for the rest of my life—and I'd just begin to nibble at my money."

RECEIVES $4,000 IN ONE DAY!

James B., an ex-insurance man, discovered 1,000 small hand looms in a rented loft. He quickly saw that big profits might be possible from the sale of such an item. He learned that the owner of the building had invented it and wanted to sell the patent. James B. bought the patent and was soon receiving 20 orders a day for the loom, which sells for $1.98.

How did he do it? By means of a small advertising brochure he had printed up, describing the loom—with a picture—giving the price, and his address. These he mailed to lists of sewing and handicrafts buyers, which he found by looking in the *Yellow Pages* of the phone directory under "Mailing Lists & List Brokers." Soon the orders came pouring in to his mailbox.

But still that's not all! Ever on the alert for free publicity, James sent his little brochures to all the big women's magazines.

Sure enough, an article on the loom appeared in *Women's Day* magazine and the orders zoomed to about 2,000 per day (roughly $4,000)! "Money consciousness" was what did it for James B.—money consciousness plus careful planning!

MAKES $25,000—IT'S AS SIMPLE AS TURNING A KNOB!

Here's another business you can start at home in your spare time—a photography studio. It's as simple as turning a knob—even simpler. Yet it can bring you up to $25,000 a year. You can run this business part time in the evenings or on Saturdays—and the beauty of it is, you don't need many customers, since you can charge up to $25 an hour!

One successful portrait photographer, Lawrence D., does all his developing and printing work in a small closet in his three-room Los Angeles apartment. His living room serves as his studio. He counts his money on the kitchen table, drives the biggest car on the block, and owns a palatial summer home on a hill overlooking a beautiful lake.

THOUSANDS OF DOLLARS A DAY—AUTOMATICALLY!

Ralph and Henry F. started a vending-machine business in their garage. Their business did so well, that today they have a modern new plant from which they control the 50,000 vending machines they have in the United States and Canada. The steady flow of pennies, nickels, dimes, and quarters has made them rich—automatically!

FINDS MAILBOX FILLED WITH MONEY!

Bill N.—always behind the eight-ball, with a wife and ten children to support—decided that he *could* succeed if he really tried. He began selling books by mail (which he picked up wholesale), in his spare time. Using the careful planning method of Psycho-Motion Pictures, he placed small ads—cautiously, at first—in local newspapers and magazines. The first month he received $26 in sales; the second month $1,012; the third month $5,118. Today, his sales volume is close to $15,000 a month!

"My mailbox is so jammed with money every week," he remarked, "I have to go to the Post Office to collect the rest of it! Almost every envelope contains cash, checks, and money orders—I pile them in stacks on the kitchen table. The total is sometimes $600-$700 a week!"

By developing a profitable mail-order product, you could do the same!

HOW TO GET MONEY QUICKLY AND EASILY

The method I am about to show you has brought new hope and happiness into the lives of millions, bringing them all the money they need to do the things they want to do. With it, you'll see . . .

* How an elderly couple instantly got the $10,000 they needed to pay off their mortgage and remodel their home!

* How a lonely, overworked, underpaid secretary got $2,500 immediately for a wonderful vacation trip to Hawaii!

* How a factory worker who was in debt automatically received enough money to pay off his bills and buy a new car, a pool, and a color TV set!

* How a grocery clerk, once doomed to a life of poverty, suddenly received $30,000 in ONE DAY, which he used to buy an apartment building!

* How a former broom-sweeper easily collected an automatic income of $23,000 a year, without working—and lives rent-free!

Here is the same technique these people used—that you can use, too—the method for obtaining personal loans!

HOW TO GET "INSTANT" PERSONAL LOANS

One of the fastest and easiest ways to get the money you need is to borrow it.

Personal loans are the easiest and fastest kind of loans to obtain, if you need money in a hurry. Since a personal loan will give you the money you need in a short time—usually within four to 24 hours—you should seriously consider it.

Using this method, you can often get up to $5,000 in one day, on your signature alone; *up to $30,000 with several signature loans on the same day!*

To obtain personal loans, check the ads in your local newspapers. You may find one or more banks advertising personal loans. Check the *Yellow Pages* of your telephone book. Most

---

*If you apply at each bank on the *same day*, then it will be true when you state in your application that you have no other loans outstanding.

banks and finance companies making personal loans will have ads in these pages. Call them and ask them to send you information.

"INSTANT MONEY" CAN BE YOURS

Loans may also be obtained from religious organizations, business firms (where you work, for example), financial brokers, insurance companies, financial advisers, and close friends. But your best bet is probably your local bank or finance company.

To qualify for a loan of $1,000 or more, you must, in general, meet these requirements: Either you or your spouse (or both) must have a steady job or own a business. You must be able to show that you have worked in one place for six months or more **(if you have not, don't worry—there's still a way)**; that you have lived in the same place for six months or more **(don't worry if you haven't—there's a way)**. You must own some kind of personal property of value. And you should be able to show that you keep your expenses at a level that is comfortably below your income.

To obtain a loan, you must start out confident that you'll get it. Your confidence radiates to the lender—he becomes so sure of you that he *wants* to lend you the money. Remember that loan officers are only human—and they respond to the simple things, the easy things that you can do to convince them to give you the money you want. When you go for a loan, ask yourself these questions:

* Are you neatly dressed?
* Are you arriving at the lender's office on time?
* Have you filled out your loan application neatly?
* Are you polite and calm at all times—even though you may be worried about getting the loan?
* Do you have a good purpose for the loan?

The most popular and most quickly approved reasons or purposes you can give for needing a loan are: medical expenses, furniture, vacation, funeral expenses, educational expenses, dental work, auto or home repairs, emergency expenses. There are hundreds of others, but these are the best.

If you are applying for a personal loan for business purposes, *do not give this as your reason.* Why? Because banks do not like to take a chance on businesses that are just starting out. Later, when you have a going business, you can apply for a *business loan*, at a much lower interest rate, and if your business is making money for you, the banks will be glad to lend you the money you need to make it grow.

Another reason you should not give for wanting a loan is back taxes. Banks and other lenders refuse to lend money for needs that recur annually—such as taxes. **You can use your money to pay your taxes** *after* **you get it** but you should not state this as your reason for wanting the money.

Above all, you must remember that if one bank turns you down, there is no reason for you to be discouraged. There is more than one bank in the world. The mere fact that one bank or lender turned you down doesn't mean the next one will. Keep looking and you're bound to succeed.

Of course, you must be certain before using this method that you will be able to repay your loan, over a period of time. If you are thinking of utilizing this money for your own spare-time business, you must make certain beforehand that you have a sure thing—a business that will pay you more than you need, to repay the loan, plus a profit. This is the careful checking process that I recommended earlier in this chapter.

RECEIVE YOUR MONEY BY MAIL!

If you are embarrassed to ask for a loan in person, you can take out a personal loan by mail. To do this, you have to know which banks and lenders make mail-order loans. The best way to do this is to check the pages of your newspaper for ads that advertise this service. If the name of the lending institution is unfamiliar to you, check with the Better Business Bureau to find out if it is a reputable one.

RECEIVE MONEY EVEN IF YOU
HAVE BEEN REFUSED BEFORE!

Some people have trouble establishing a credit rating—which means proof, to the bank's satisfaction, that you will be capable of repaying the loan. To remedy this:

(1) Establish a permanent address, if you have moved around a lot Check with friends or relatives, to find out if they will let you use theirs.

(2) Be ready to show that you have a *permanent* occupation of some sort. Notice, I didn't say full time. It can be a spare-time business that you have engaged in from time to time, on your own. Even if you were just *thinking* of starting such a business you can give it as your permanent occupation. Have a business name and address ready, if someone asks, and be ready to speak of future plans for this business. (You need not tell the bank if your business earned little or no profits.)

(3) Try to make your income look as high as possible. If you are married—and both of you work—include your spouses's income. Add all other income, including the earnings of a son or daughter who is living with you, loan payments made to you, and bank interest. Remember, you do not have to mention the source of all your income—just the total amount.

HOW TO MAKE A LOAN OFFICER
INSTANTLY APPROVE YOUR LOAN

Let's say you have followed all these steps, and the lender still turns you down. He says your income is insufficient. What do you do? You ask the bank if it will accept a co-signer. This will often make a loan official say "yes" instead of "no." For example:

You go into a bank for a loan. The credit man scowls at you and says: "Got a co-signer?" You say, "No." He frowns and says: "Sorry, you don't qualify for a loan." Quickly you say: "Yes, but I can get one!" It's like using an Insta-Matic Psycho-Command or Spell, a brain-wave sender! In a flash, his tune changes. He smiles at you—suddenly—and says: "On the other hand, if you can get one, we'll be happy to give you $1,000 more than you asked for. Any time you want more, just see me personally, and we'll avoid all that paperwork. Thank you so much for coming by."

It's as simple as that!

What is a co-signer? Where can you find one? A co-signer is someone who signs the application with you.

Now, your co-signer may be earning even less than you. However, this doesn't matter, as long as both your incomes together add up to enough. Typical acceptable co-signers include: brother, sister, father, mother, cousin, aunt, uncle, friends. Use only as many as the bank requires—no more. The co-signer signs his name with yours and agrees to share responsibility, but this is seldom a problem between close friends or relatives. If it is a problem, you can remedy it by *paying* someone to act as your co-signer. This is done quite often, and it is legal.

It actually costs you nothing to pay him, since you are going to pay him with a small part of your borrowed money, usually 1 to 5 per cent.

You can advertise for a co-signer in the classified section of your local newspaper.

HOW TO GET MONEY THAT DOESN'T HAVE TO BE REPAID!

There are many other types of loans—other than the personal loans which we have just discussed. Some of them bring more money and are fairly easy to get (but not as easy as the personal loan, which requires no collateral). All of them have one thing in common, however—they must be repaid.

All except one, which I am about to reveal to you . . . And that is a stock offering! You can sell stocks, which are shares or part ownership of your spare-time business, and this money:

* Doesn't have to be repaid!
* Is interest-free!
* Is tax-free!
* Can be used for any business purpose!
* Will pay *your* salary!
* Can be used to repay loans!

This secret may contain the key to great wealth for you. It can put money in your business bank account quickly and with little effort on your part. Even if your business is brand new, and you haven't made one sale yet, you can still sell stock in your company. You need not even have an office (your home address can be used if you don't yet have a business address). You can go on selling stock in your business for years and years, and the money received is tax-free. Since you are the president of your own company, you can sell stock to the public without the need of a stockbroker. In this manner, you may raise any amount you wish, up to $1 million or more, and form as many companies as you wish.

To sell stock, you must register your company with your state as a corporation. Do not let the word "corporation" fool you or frighten you. It is a relatively simple matter to become the owner of a corporation. Simply write to the Office of the Director, Department of Taxation and Finance (you'll find the address in your phone book, under the name of your state) and ask for information as to what steps to take—the procedure varies from state to state. In some states, for example, a lawyer is not necessary, and you may incorporate the business yourself simply by filling out the necessary forms and paying the required fees. In other states, you may need a lawyer. In fact, it is wise—as a general rule—to hire a lawyer to incorporate your business for you, whether you need one or not.

The cost of incorporating your business varies from state to state, the smallest amount you may be required to spend being as little as $50. This is for the state registration fee, the notary fee, state tax on stock, postage, corporate forms, and seal. And you'd be surprised at how many "little" businesses—people you deal with every day—are incorporated.

You say you don't have a dime? Then borrow the money you need, and repay your lenders using corporate cash obtained from your stock offering. It doesn't have to cost you a cent.

A FORTUNE SECRET THAT PAYS OFF BIG!

Do you desire an attractive home or apartment? A car of your choice? A hobby you enjoy? High-class vacations? Clothes? The best that money can buy? Wealth? Leisure? Luxuries? You can, with a positive mental attitude and the hints given in these pages, enjoy all these things and more. Others have done it. So can you!

In every case, the money you get with this method can bring you the things you desire. In every case, all the things you ask for can appear—or materialize—seemingly out of "nothingness" with Psycho-Command and the Supreme Command of self-confidence.

Psycho-Command Power #6

HOW TO MAKE OTHERS "LOVE SLAVES" TO YOUR MAGNETIC "LOVE PULL"

What would you give for a magic love spell that would make you irresistible to any man or woman of your choice? A magic love spell that would instantly fill your entire being with an enormous, magnetic "love pull" to open their minds and hearts to you.

This Magic Love Spell could be used to bring your mate to you without asking, and make him or her voluntarily do the things you have longed for, even if you haven't looked at each other in years! It could bring back harmony and cooperation to a troubled marriage—and even more, so powerful would be its spell that it would charm and enchant all those you wanted it to ... your spouse or child, neighbor, co-worker, boss, even people you never met before!

FAMOUS LOVE SPELLS

Would it surprise you to learn that there actually *is* such a Love Spell—albeit different than you may have thought. Traditionally, love spells have been shrouded in mystery and mysticism.

In ancient Greece, Hecate was considered the

goddess of love, and in her honor many ceremonies were performed. The magician practiced extreme chastity, and while preparing for the rites rigorously fasted, taking frequent baths and anointing his body with oils.

For the actual ceremony, he wore a white robe, without any knot or fastening, and adorned with purple streamers, and it was essential that he should have complete faith in the powers. The ceremony was performed only at sunrise or sunset.

To incite love, a famous love charm was used—a ceremony known as "Drawing Down the Moon," in the process of which Hecate was invoked, and an image of clay imbued with a spirit which was bidden to go forth and fetch the desired man or woman.

Still secretly practiced today, the preliminaries included burning vervain and frankincense, followed by a solemn chant so powerful it was believed capable of calling down the moon. Around an image of the loved one, ribbons of three colors were wound three times, while the words, "Thus I bind the fillets of Venus" were chanted, and the figure was carried around an altar. After this, it was set before the altar—and two more images, one of wax and one of clay, were placed in the fire of the altar. As the figure of clay hardened, so did the heart that was sought. As the figure of wax softened, so was the heart of the loved one made tender.

The Goddess Hecate was invoked to possess the first image and to go forth to entice the desired woman. A sacred cake was broken over this, and laurels were burnt before it.

Another powerful love spell was to make two figures of wax or clay—one representing the god Ares, and another a woman. The male figure stood facing the woman, pointing a sword at her throat. The figure of the woman (or man), knelt with its hands tied behind its back. On the limbs of the kneeling figure were written names of demons, and 13 bronze needles were stuck into it. The lover meanwhile recited: "I pierce her (his) heart" (or whatever part of the body was being stuck) "that she (he) may think of me." These words were then inscribed upon a metal plate, and tied to the wax figures, together with a string knotted 365 times. After this, both figures were buried at a crossroads.

The powdered roots of the male and female mandrake were, and still are, used to incite love in many European countries. The powder was burned over a fire with some of the operator's pubic hair and characteristic secretions. At the same time, the desire of the operator was uttered, invoking a demon to draw the desired person to the operator's abode.

Hindu women make a powder of an aphrodisiacal nature by frying the genital organs of male turtles, together with love chants.

In Italy, on Midsummer's Night, many Christian peasants gather garlic onions. Little feasts are made of the boiled vegetables, as it is believed to incite desire for love. In the Middle Ages, for the maid who wished to bind her lover to her forever, there was the *confarreaties*—a confection made of flour, honey, seeds, excreta, and/or menstrual blood.

In Africa, there is a thriving trade in rhinoceros horn. Rhino horn dust was highly regarded as an aphrodisiac, and was believed to be one of the strongest that it was possible to use.*

THE GREATEST LOVE SPELL OF ALL

And yet, despite all the strange superstitions and unusual practices with which the world abounds, the greatest love secret of them all has yet to be mentioned.

It is the magic love potion that wizards and wise men were rumored to have discovered, in ancient times. Surely you've heard of it—a magic "mixture" you could drink, or give to others, that would immediately draw others to you, fill them with the spirit of kindness and understanding, and in effect make them "love slaves" to your "magnetic love pull." A "wonder drug" for love that would act like a powerful Love Magnet.

Solomon, the wisest man of his time, and possibly of all time, hinted at it in the Song of Solomon. Homer and Virgil wrote odes about it. And Ovid's Magic Love Formula is reputed

---

*Doctors consider it a harmful irritant, however. In the United States, wine mixed with roe, or champagne served with caviar were said to be aphrodisiacs. Millet cereal, licorice, and sarsaparilla tea have been praised as love foods. There is no scientific verification of this, however.

to reveal the secret. Casanova and Don Juan knew it well. For it makes you *seem* like a different person—and others *see* that you are different, sense your inner strength, and look to you as the genuinely spiritual person they hoped existed all along. You will be the one person for whom they have been searching all their lives.

Not for over a thousand years has a magic adept been willing to set it down in writing, however. Can it be they feared it would unloose the uncontrollable love urges of millions upon millions of men and women? The time has come, I feel, to *let the people know*, and fill the world with love and happiness, instead of hatred and war. And so I am about to reveal it to you.

Drink of this knowledge, and you will indeed have quaffed the legendary, true *Magic Love Potion*.

Love Spell #1—A Secret Love Potion

The formula for this Magic Love Potion may be summed up in these words:

"Give, and it shall be given unto you; good measure, pressed down, and shaken together, and running over, shall men give unto your bosom. For with the same measure that ye mete withal it shall be measured to you again."—Luke 6:38.

Real love is GIVING. It seeks only the good of the loved one. Who are the unhappiest creatures on earth? Not the poor or the sick—but those who keep all their love for themselves.

"Giving? To get love? I don't quite understand," you say. Perhaps not, but let me explain.

Who are the people that you like? Isn't it true that the people you like best are the ones who seem to like you? Who seem always to be concerned about how you feel, and what they can do for you? Who smile pleasantly whenever you greet them, who always have a pleasant word for you? Who try to make you laugh? And who seem to enjoy your company— regardless of how grouchy you may be? Who always seem ready to listen to your problems and lend a sympathetic hand if they can? Who even make you feel a little guilty and indebted to them *because* of their friendship, their concern?

What have they done to *make* you like them? They have given! They have simply given of themselves!

You may say, "Yes, this is true. I have a friend or two like this, but I don't actually *love* them. It's the person that I *love* who doesn't seem to care about me. What shall I do?"

That brings us to the second ingredient of this Magic Love Potion: how to inspire love in another. Read carefully. Drink of this knowledge, and you must succeed!

HOW TO MAKE YOUR SECRET DESIRES COME TRUE

How to inspire love in another? First by cultivating it in yourself. Love *begets* love. Charge yourself with unselfish love and devotion. *Give* without any thought of receiving, and the seeds of love which you have planted will blossom with a harvest of their own kind. For there is an unwritten Law of the Universe: for every action there is a response, a return of the pendulum that we have started swinging. Above all, you must seek only the good of the ones you love.

Deviate from this course, and you will be detected. Deviate from this course, and you will be undone. For love is *giving*. It cannot be jealous. It must seek only the good of the one loved. "Blessed is he that truly loves and seeketh not love in return," said St. Francis ". . . that serves and desires not to be served . . . that doeth good unto others and seeketh not that others do good unto him."

Love Spell# 2—Turning Hate to Love

Love is both spiritual and physical. The love that exists between young boys and girls is the primal Earth love, urging us to procreate.

True spiritual love is based on many things. The capacity to be unselfish, to wish good fortune to the loved ones, no matter at what cost to the lover, to serve the loved one and to humble oneself.

Many men will contend that they are loving, when all that they are is jealous and possessive; loving their wives and children as they do their other possessions, and valuing them more like things than people. The proof that many a man and woman is the mere possessor is shown when the person whom they say they love deserts them for another. Then their alleged love turns to hate. A true lover, under such circumstances, can be grieved and bereft, but cannot hate.

HYPNOTIC LOVE POWER

What is Hypnotic Love Power? Read the section on Miracle Magnetism and you will see. It is that "something" in the glance of the eyes, the turn of the head, the touch of the hand, that sends an electric thrill through every fiber of the one at whom it is directed. Hypnotic Love Power is the taking of the gifts God has given you and using them, in the service or pleasure of others. It is being so full of the appreciation of life . . . that even poor features are lost sight of in the dazzle of your charm.

Was Bogart handsome? Or Garfield? Or Cagney? Of course not. Take the fascinating women of history—Cleopatra, the Queen of Sheba, Catherine the Great, Helen of Troy—none of them had beautiful features. Cleopatra's nose was much too big, and yet she held Caesar, the ruler of the world, spellbound for ten long years. And after that, Mark Anthony.

What they had—joy, mystery, charm—they gave, and received love in return, a hundred, a thousandfold.

STRANGE "LOVE GAMES" YOU CAN PLAY

To make your secret desires come true, just ask yourself— What have I to GIVE that will add to the happiness of those around me, especially the person whose love I desire?

Whatever that may be—a pleasant word, a kindly smile, a happy thought—*give* it. As fast as each new opportunity presents itself to give happiness to someone else, USE it. Make this your goal, and you will be surprised how many simple little ways there are of brightening the lives of others, as well as your own. Call them "Love Games" or "Magic Love Spells," if you will.

You can use these "Love Spells" in the home, in business, in whatever you are doing and wherever you are working. It may sound strange, but you must give to get. You must sow the seed, before you can reap the harvest.

Love Spell #3—How to Catch and Hold a Man

"I learned how to control a man from my mother-in-law,"* says Betty Jo. "Shortly after we were married, my husband and I had the usual disenchantment most young couples encounter, and since my own mother had died in my early childhood, I had to turn to my mother-in-law for help. Thank God for her understanding . . ."

In brief, she told Betty Jo to be a good listener, a good lover, and to make her man feel important by showering him with attention, every chance she got. "Do this," she said, "and your husband will be true to you all his life!"

"And my friend, that's so," says Betty Jo. "I have 30 years of marriage to prove it. Maybe he looked at another woman now and then, but only with his left eye. He kept his right on me all the time!"

GOING "ALL THE WAY" WITH A MAN

There is no faster way on earth of driving someone away from you than by constantly talking about yourself. Not even your best friend can put up with never ending stories about yourself. The only way you can win lasting love and friendship with someone is to become truly interested in his or her problems. And the only way to do this is to listen. Listening shows that you care, and makes the other person feel important.

Here's how one girl has made practical use of this secret: "A lot of girls think that if you're going to be popular with the fellows and get a lot of dates, you've got to go all the way with him,"† says Marion H. "That's not true at all. My phone is

---

*Reported by James K. Van Fleet, in *Power with People* (West Nyack, N.Y.: Parker Publishing Co., Inc., 1969).

†Ibid.

always ringing and I have a lot more offers for a date than I can accept. What's my secret? It's simple, really. I use only four words, and I have never had to sit at home alone yet. All I say to a man is—*'Tell me about yourself!'* And he does—and loves it, too!"

Love Spell #4—For a Happy Marriage

If you want to maintain a harmonious relationship in your home, then all you need to do is give your wife or husband the love and attention he or she deserves and craves. You don't have to send your wife flowers or candy every day, for example, to show her how much you appreciate her. Here is a method that costs you absolutely nothing, and is even more effective.

Pay attention to her. Let her know by your actions that your know she's around. Say *please* and *thank you* to her when you want something. And if you enjoy the meals she has prepared, *tell* her about it. She won't know unless you do. And when you pass by her, reach out and brush her hand gently, once in a while. Or bring her a cup of tea or coffee in the afternoon.

These may sound like tiny, inconsequential things—but they serve as positive proof to your wife that you still love her and that you still appreciate her. And she'll return that love to you, because she will not want to lose it.

One man who does this never gives his wife any presents— except on her birthday, their anniversary, and Christmas—and yet he and his wife have been happily married for 30 years!

PSYCHO-MOTION PICTURE FOR LOVE

Start planning today to use this Magic Love Formula in your daily life. Simply drink of the secret knowledge this potion gives you to make your dreams come true.

Say, for example, that you want to attract a certain member of the opposite sex, silently, by unobserved means, without being obvious.

First of all, using the technique of Psycho-Motion Pictures (*planning*), you would choose, out of all the attractive men or women you see, the one most desirable to you. Next, you would observe all the qualities which he or she possesses. Look at this person intently, from time to time, without making him or her feel uncomfortable. Try to get the "feel" of this person's personality, how he or she walks, talks, moves, reacts to different situations, his or her temperament, likes and dislikes.

Finally, when you are completely "attuned" to this person, simply relax, sit back, and let your mind dwell upon all the ways you can make yourself attractive to this person. Try to think of the things that would be attractive to *you*, if you were this person.

Are you normally expressionless, or frowning, when you are around other people? If so, resolve here and now, to smile and be cheerful whenever you meet this person. Nod, raise your hand in greeting, say "Hello!" as you walk by. If this person responds, take the slightest opportunity to say something else—remark on the weather, if you are out-of-doors, or the fact that you have a rush errand, or that you are looking for someone or something (even if you need no directions)—anything at all—and do this sort of thing the next few times you meet this person, just to get him or her used to talking to you.

Do not be discouraged if this person does not respond immediately. Persist in your efforts, and you will be rewarded with success.

When you have reached the stage where both of you are quite accustomed to saying hello, try to prolong these little conversations. Exchange pleasantries, or perhaps even a joke, or make a humorous remark about yourself, to show that you are only human. As you get to know this person, show more and more interest in him or her, by inquiring about what this person happens to be doing, how he or she likes living (or working) in this particular place, what problems he or she has, offering sympathy or helpful suggestions if you can.

At this point, if you are a man, you may suggest an evening out for dinner or a movie. And whether you are a man or woman, if you should happen to see this person where you work, during lunch, for example, you may seat yourself at the same table. Always strive to be at or near a place where this person happens to be. If you work in the same place, and you are a woman, for example, you can easily stop by and chat without embarrassment, as often as you wish. Once you have become very close friends, if you have matrimony in mind, and the other person has not responded warmly enough—you may use this simple method of jolting the other person into a realization of what he or she must do: suddenly, and without warning, withdraw your attention. Stay away from this person for a brief time—say, a few days, a week or so. And when he or she appears, and asks what's the matter, say little except that you thought he or she was angry at you. This alone will often serve to redouble this person's desire to please you and make you happy. It can lead to love, marriage, or a real and lasting friendship—whatever you desire.

For other tricks which you may use, to encourage the reaction you desire from someone else, see pages 30-33 ("Hypnotic Commands"), page 34 ("The Secret of Speed Hypnosis"), pages 41-42 ("The Miracle Magnet"), page 42 ("Secrets of Silent Command"), page 39 ("How to Make Someone More Affectionate").

THE MAN WHO WALKED OUT OF
THE PHOTOGRAPH!

Julie K., 48, was a widow, but still "looking." Widowed early in life, she had no family, no children, and was desperately lonely. She had taken to joining social clubs and wearing "friendship" rings, but she was miserable and had no one to comfort her.

One day, while reading the newspapers, she happened to notice a photograph of an old school chum, Martin T., a man whom she had dated many years before. He looked a little older, of course, with slightly greying temples, but he was still handsome. The caption underneath the photo said that he was the newly elected president of a local civic group, that he had beening living in a nearby town for many years, and that he had been actively engaged in local charities ever since his wife had passed on, she too having been engaged in these same charities.

Using The Supreme Command of self-confidence, Julie K. began planning the steps she would take to renew her acquaintance with this man—silently, by unobserved means, without seeming obvious. She began attending meetings of his particular civic group, seating herself in the front row seat where he could see her, hoping that this would stir his memory.

After several meetings, by which time she had joined the group and become a committee member, he approached her and said, "I hope you'll forgive my boldness, but I just can't help feeling I know you. Did you, by any chance, ever go to school in Evansville?" Now Julie knew the spell was operating.

Soon they began reminiscing about their high school days and the events that had taken place since then. He asked her to dinner, became a frequent caller on the telephone, and they became quite good friends.

Finally, one day, after a dinner date and a movie, he turned to her in the car, and told her how much he missed her all week long. He told her how lonely he was, and how much he loved her, and asked her if she would have him as her husband. Julie smiled, through tear-blurred eyes, and nodded her approval. "Yes, I love you too," she said.

Now, together and happily married, their life has been one of harmony and bliss. Martin T. had, in effect, walked out of the photograph and into Julie's life! He was exactly what she had envisioned in every respect!

SPOUSE BEGS TO RETURN

Michael E. thought he was happily married, until he discovered that his wife was seeing another man. And yet he still loved her, and he wanted desperately to hold their little family together. "I can and will succeed," he stated.

With this Supreme Command, he began planning the steps that would bring her back. Without letting on that he knew anything about her affair, he began to fill his entire mind with thoughts of love, admiration, appreciation, and forgiveness for Betty, his wife. Over and over he kept saying to himself, "What have I to *give* her that will make her happy and rekindle the fires of love in her heart for me?"

He began doing things for her, running errands, doing chores, showering her with words of love, gifts, and affection. He made their home so warm and full of love that Betty began to feel guilty about leaving him. She was so ashamed, in fact, that she hadn't the heart to tell him what she'd been meaning to tell him for months.

Instead, she began seeing less and less of her boyfriend. Then, suddenly, without warning, Michael confronted her with the evidence he had discovered. Why had she done it? How could she do it? Why? Why? Why? He told her he was deeply hurt and couldn't understand it. Perhaps, if she felt that way, she better leave.

Stunned, Betty pleaded with Michael to take her back, and begged tearfully to be forgiven. Michael sulked a bit, but then, after a while, he said softly that he still loved her and that he was willing to try again if she was. They hugged and made up, and Michael knew that the spell was working, and that she would never leave him again.

HUSBAND STOPS DRINKING

Ellen E. reported that her husband did nothing but sit around all day and drink beer. He lost his job and felt he was too old to start again. That was his reason, he said. He would whine and complain all day, leaving the house only to collect his unemployment check—and then he would come home late, staggering in drunk. He was unclean, unshaven, and spent most of his time staring out the window. He stashed bottles around the house, no matter how many times Ellen cleaned and threw them out. He developed a peculiar hand tremor (nerves, he called it), and almost overnight began to look and act like an old man. His speech became garbled, his memory hazy, he had a big beer belly (he had gained 50 lbs.)—and, although only 54, showed all the signs of early senility.

Ellen was worried sick. Just to look at him was making a nervous wreck out of her. Finally, after hearing about this method, she began planning her strategy. Using the Magic Love Formula of this chapter, she began methodically "giving" of herself in such a way that it literally shamed her husband, Ed, into snapping out of it and getting hold of himself.

The first thing Ellen did was to get a job, during the day, as a secretary. But, in addition, she also took a second job, in the evening, as a waitress. This caused her to come home, tired and wan-looking, only for brief intervals. Soon Ed realized that he was hardly seeing anything of her. And during the weekends, Ellen was so tired, she slept till noon, and sometimes longer.

Ed was soon forced to do housework he had never done before. He had to wash the dishes; make the beds; prepare breakfast, lunch, and supper for his wife; shop; and take care of the children.

And whenever he left the house, he had to face the scornful glances of the neighbors. Even when he stopped at the local tavern for a drink, his friends moved away from him and made snide remarks about men who take money from women.

This made Ed angry—so angry that he resolved then and there to find a job and put an end to this nonsense. Day after day, he left the children with neighbors and went out looking for work, until he finally landed a good job as a construction crewman.

And, without even realizing it, Ed had overcome his drinking problem, voluntarily! Lately, he hadn't even had *time* for a nip! Soon his tremors disappeared, his mind became sharp and clear, his excess pounds began slipping away—he felt young, and healthy, completely rejuvenated, almost overnight! Ellen was able to give up both her jobs, and she knew that once again their lives would be happy.

LOVE CONQUERS ALL

Love is like a magnet. Like the magnet of iron which gives off electricity, and—by its very giving—draws to itself its own. When all its power has gone, like a magnet, it has only to rub against a stronger magnet to be renewed.

Love gives out a current of love, and all who come within its reach are attracted to it. A selfish man, a jealous man, an angry man has no magnetism. He repels everyone he comes in contact with. Because real love is *giving*.

So if you want to receive something good, show your love by GIVING. It doesn't matter how poor you are, how much in debt. You can always give something. Remember that giving increases after its kind, so give of what you want to receive, whether it be love, service, or money.

Psycho-Command Power #7

HOW TO SEE BEYOND
CLOSED DOORS!
"Love Fever" and the Secretly
Passionate Man or Woman

I want to tell you about a "secret window" you can look through—that tells you many things about others. An actual "secret window" that lets you see past the closed doors of their minds, see what they are really thinking and doing.

This secret window is revealed with paper. For when a person writes, he leaves actual pictures that reveal what he is thinking. These pictures tell many tales beyond mere words. They reveal his thoughts and desires—what he has done in the past, what he is secretly doing now, what he will do in the future.

What's more, this secret window lets you see up close—even at a distance of many miles—as through "magic mental binoculars." For even a simple letter or postcard from someone (unknown to him) can be like a television camera planted in his very home, transmitting pictures to you.

A PSYCHIC WINDOW MORE POWERFUL
THAN A CRYSTAL BALL

Your handwriting is a reflection of your personality. From the depths of the mind an impulse flows to the hand revealing *pictures* of your hidden thoughts—as clear as life, and plain as day, to anyone who knows the secrets that open this psychic window!

Are you one of those people who doesn't believe in handwriting analysis? Do you regard it as mere fortune-telling? Well, I don't believe in fortune-telling by handwriting, either. Handwriting analysis is not fortune-telling. It is a proven, scientific procedure for determining what is on a person's mind.

It is an accepted method, used today by large corporations, physicians, psychologists, and psychiatrists, to determine people's talents, needs, desires, and personality—the things they are likely to do in any situation—just as the Rorschach ink blot test and the word-association test (made famous by Carl G. Jung) are also commonly used.

The things a person puts on a piece of paper are done unconsciously, just as certain body motions are made without realizing it. In fact, handwriting is just another form of Body Language.

TELL-TALE SIGNS TO LOOK FOR

Whatever traits you show in ordinary, everyday life, you will show through in handwriting. If you move slowly, speak slowly, and are a slow, deliberate thinker—careful in all that you do—these habits will show up in your handwriting, in the careful way you dot your *i*'s and cross your *t*'s, the care you take in forming all your letters, regardless of how bad you are at spelling.

If you walk quickly, talk quickly, think fast, eat fast, drive fast, and are habitually hasty in all that you do—these traits will all show themselves in your hasty handwriting. An *m* may be written so hastily that it will look like a straight line—with maybe a slight squiggle—instead of two carefully drawn humps.

Fig. 1

If you are hasty in all that you do, you will probably forget to dot your *i*'s or cross some of your *t*'s. You may be good at spelling, but if you are hasty you may find that you misspell words that you know, out of sheer haste or impatience.

If you suffer from fatigue, physical exhaustion, or lack of energy—these will show up in your pen pressure, which will not be very great. Your writing will also tend to go downhill as your arm tires. If you are highly energetic, have drive, enthusiasm aggressiveness—these will show up in your pen pressure, too, which will be very heavy.

A WOMAN WHO IS DISAPPOINTED
IN MARRIAGE

If you are a woman who is, by nature, proud and self-confident—but who has been disappointed in marriage—your signature may show a large first letter in your own name, and a smaller first letter in your married name. (See Fig. 1.)

A WOMAN WHO FEELS INFERIOR
TO HER HUSBAND

If you are a woman who is proud of her husband—and even feel inferior to him in some way—you may find that the first letter of your first name is smaller than the first letter of his name, your married name. (See Fig. 2.)

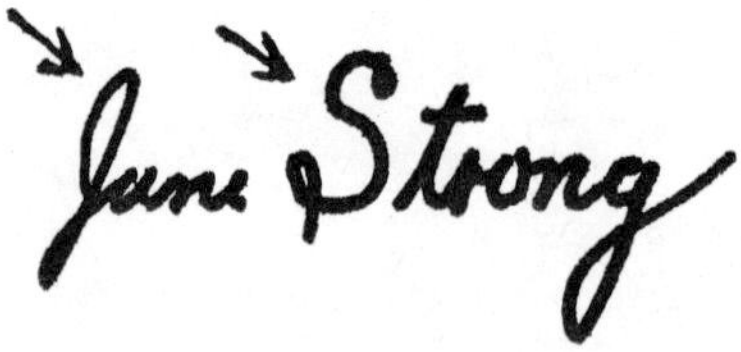

Fig. 2

A FREE-LIVER
—OR BIG SPENDER

If you are the type of person who enjoys all the comforts of life—and refuse to deny yourself in any way—if you are a free spender, who likes to live life on a big scale, enjoy eating, drinking, and entertainment, and let the future take care of itself (in other words, if you have trouble saving money), this may show up in your handwriting in the way you tend to waste space on the paper, taking perhaps two pages to write what could have fit on one page. There will be wide spaces between your letters and words—double spaces between your lines. (See Fig. 3.)

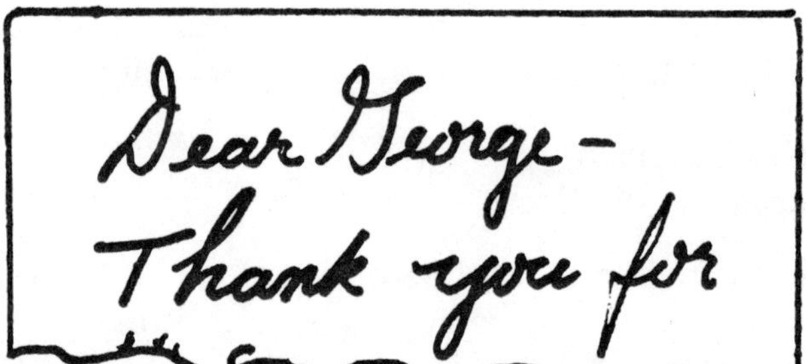

Fig. 3

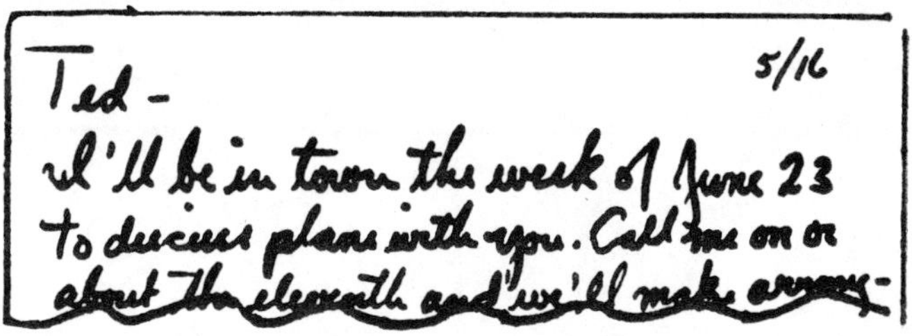
Ted - 5/16
I'll be in town the week of June 23
to discuss plans with you. Call me on or
about the eleventh and we'll make arrang-

Fig. 4

THE SLY PERSON

On the other hand, if you are a careful saver, a careful planner, with an eye out for the future, your handwriting will tend to be small—you will tend to save space on the paper by writing your letters closer together and making the space between lines smaller. You will tend to start near the edge of one side of the page and write until you reach the other side. (Fig. 4.)

And if you are torn between saving and spending, if you have undergone years of sacrifice and self-denial, have had enough of it, and feel that now, perhaps, it is time to start enjoying yourself—your writing may be larger. Or it may still be small, but you may leave a lot of space on either side of the paper and between the lines.

* * * * * *

But the size and shape of your handwriting reveal even more intimate details than this brief glimpse has given you. Handwriting is like a secret window that lets you see through the closed doors of other people's minds.

As a long-practicing graphologist—or handwriting analyst—I have endeavored to set down in this chapter the fundamental principles of the science of graphology, so that all who desire may learn how they, too, can read character in handwriting.

The Love Meter

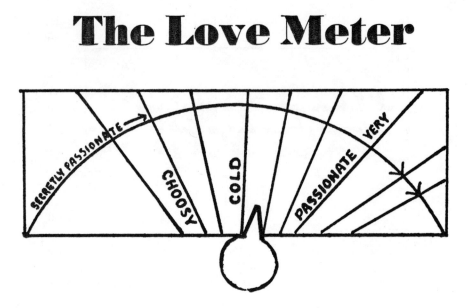

Fig. 5 *Which way does your handwriting slant?*

A LOVE METER THAT SHOWS YOU
AFFECTION IN OTHERS

Just as a Geiger counter can be used by fortune hunters to detect uranium, so there is a way by which the amount of affection in others can be detected. I refer, of course, to handwriting, which can actually be a kind of Love Meter or Love Machine, that beats as loudly or softly as the heart itself. If you look at the Love Meter on this page, you will see what I mean.

This Love Meter shows three basic types of writing: (1) upright, (2) left-leaning, and (3) right-leaning. The meaning* of these slants is clear.

That meaning, simply stated, is this: writing that slants to the right represents a leaning toward people, and writing that

---

*Every book on handwriting analysis devotes at least one chapter to the inclination of the letters, and all the experts, such as Ulrich Sonnemann, Ph.D., Irene Marcuse, Ph.D., H. Falcon, Ph.D., Robert Saudek, Ph.D., and others, agree as to the meaning of these slants.

slants to the left* represents a leaning away from people. Writing that is straight up and down indicates no particular leaning either way.

That is why the Love Meter shows three main categories. When you use the Love Meter in Fig. 5, you must remember two things: (1) the slant of the writing represents the *frequency* with which you express your emotions, and (2) the amount of pressure in writing indicates the *intensity* of these emotions.

HOW THE LOVE METER SHOWS "PASSION" IN OTHERS

Let us say the majority of letters written by the person you are curious about slant to the right—indicating "Passionate" on the Love Meter. Such a heavy slant forward represents basically outgoing emotions, expressed often and with enthusiasm. It indicates that the writer leans *toward people*, emotionally.

Perhaps you can get a clearer idea of this from an example in a book called *Self-Knowledge Through Handwriting*† by the late Hans J. Jacoby: "A man who is carried away by the speaker will lean forward as if wanting to meet him; another, by leaning back, seems to recoil from him in an effort to escape and ward off his influences; the upright position shows neither sympathy with the lecturer nor its opposite—it is the attitude of the self-sufficient person."

I repeat, now, that *most* of the letters must slant in one direction, to give you a true reading. (If all the letters slant every which way, it indicates confusion.) If most of the letters slant in one direction, this gives you the writer's *habitual* pattern of emotional expression. Dr. Falcon†† calls this the

---

*Many people seem to think that left-handed writing is only done by left-handed people. In fact, they think that left-handed people write no other way. This is completely false. Many right-handers write slanting left. If the writer is permitted to move the paper around to any position that pleases him, he will get any slant he desires.

†Hans J. Jacoby, *Self-Knowledge Through Handwriting* (London, England: Dent & Sons, Ltd., 1941).

††Hal Falcon, *How to Analyze Handwriting* (New York, N.Y.: Cornerstone Library, 1964).

person's "E.Q." (Emotion Quotient) or "Love-Fever," the degree of emotion this person shows.

The Love Meter shows three main categories: (1) *Passionate* (slanting right), (2) *Cold* (upright), (3) *Self-Centered* (slanting left). Now let us see, specifically, what the first of these, the *Passionate* slant, means.

(1) "Passionate" Handwriting

The more handwriting leans to the right, the greater the degree of affection the writer possesses. Handwriting that leans to the right indicates great ardor and the capacity for expressing it. Such people are outgoing, gregarious, they like people, and they tend to show it. It is a curious fact that even the Chinese have a saying: "He whose writing leans to the right is as a reed bent by the wind of love." (Normally, Chinese writing does not lean at all!)

The more the handwriting leans to the right, the more the writer demands of life. People with this extreme forward-leaning tendency in writing are seldom satisfied with plain comfort, but want luxury, personal ease, and some of the exotic pleasures. They like to spend money for pleasure—are generous, too—and are more or less ruled by their senses, though not necessarily coarse or sordid. The harder the pressure, the more "passionate" they tend to be.

They make good salespeople, managers, personnel directors, counselors—anything to do with people, because they like people and get along well with others. They tend to get very enthusiastic about anything they believe in, and this enthusiasm rubs off on others. For this reason, they make good fund-raisers, and are unsurpassed as salesmen.

The more this forward-leaning writing comes upward, however, the more restrained—even cold—these people tend to be. They may enjoy face-to-face contact with people, for example, but prefer to stay in the office as managers. This "mildly passionate" type writing belongs to the auditor, the investigator, the scientist, the business executive. The harder the pressure, the more successful the person. Justice is as important to this type of person as truth, and whenever he sees injustice done to anyone, he is among the first to speak out.

The more this "passionate" handwriting slants to the right, however, the more fun-loving and outgoing the person is. People like this should not play poker—because what they feel is often written all over their faces.

(2) "Cold" Handwriting

Upright handwriting tends to show an extremely "cold" personality (although the person himself might be the first to deny it). Such writers, it has been found, almost dislike the open display of affection. They are indifferent to caresses, and show what they feel only by the fact that they are attentive to certain people and inattentive to others.

Nearly all upright writing has large, rather round, and carefully made letter formations. These are the people who are orderly, sensible, and self-governed. They are also very careful—one might even say "tight" or "close-fisted"—with money. They are good savers and generally think twice before spending any money. They will, however, spend—lavishly, on occasion—on things which are important to *them*. If this were a woman's script, and especially if the pressure were light, she would probably be the kind who would marry late or not at all. She would probably be a professional musician, librarian, teacher, secretary, or just plain "working woman"—but she would almost certainly *want* to be "independent."

Because of their calm, logical minds—and ability to weigh facts without getting emotionally involved—men in this category make good doctors, researchers, investigators, or businessmen, especially if the pressure is heavy.

People of this nature are very efficient and are especially good at routine. They ask little from life, except relative peace, quiet, and contentment.

(3) "Choosy" Writing

Handwriting that leans to the left shows coolness—but of a different kind. Like the "passionate" writer, these writers *feel* the extremes of emotion—love, hate, anger, joy—but tend to suppress these feelings greatly.

This backhand type of writing always indicates repression of some sort—even in left-handed people, who give this as an excuse. Backhand writers, as a rule, are timid about showing either love or hate. They are self-conscious in manner, and do not express what they feel with any ease. They are always looking *inward*, examining and criticizing themselves. They think others are examining and "talking" about them, too. They are sensitive and quick to take offense at harmless remarks, thinking—mistakenly—that others are making fun of them.

They are choosy and selfish about anything that seems important to them—clothes, cars, home furnishings and drapery, tools, possessions, and especially friends. These people select their friends with utmost care, have very few *real* friends, and are often loners.

In the company of others, they seek approval. They want very much to please. They are good actors, and what they say is often not what they feel. They tell people what they like to hear in order to "get along."

They are often alone, without being lonely. Many of them, in fact, insist on having privacy, a place where they can be alone—even away from members of their own family, whom they love—a private boudoir, den, or study. This is a quality shared by all creative people and with most geniuses.

People whose handwriting slants to the left often show small, very carefully made letters. They are generally good with money (not necessarily "cheap," but "careful") or anything that has to do with figures. They are good planners—always with an eye out for every contingency—and make good scientists, technicians, bankers, businessmen, or investment experts.

The larger the letters, the more artistic (and free with money) such people tend to be—singers, dancers, artists, musicians, actors and actresses, fashion designers, or decorators. Pressure is very important, in this case. The heavier the pressure, the more likely it is that the person actually is in one of these occupations. The lighter the pressure, the more likely it is that the person is a dreamer, who would like to do these things but can never "find time." If such a person needs to support his- or herself, he or she will take the first job available and then complain about it.

When left-leaning writing slants all the way to the left—especially with large, scrawling letters—we have a highly emotional person with fewer restraints. He is more like the forward-leaning writer, in that he likes people, is interested in them—and is basically affectionate—but he is apt to get into arguments over petty things and lose friends.

SECRETLY "PASSIONATE" PEOPLE

The third slant, which we have just discussed—the left-leaning or "Self-Centered" one—is very interesting. People with this form of handwriting are often the ones who look as if they had never heard of love, but their eyes betray them to anyone who is accustomed to reading faces, just as their handwriting betrays them to the graphologist.

These people are not philanderers, and often are capable of the deepest and most absolutely unselfish devotion, but they are always jealous and passionate.

Men with this type of writing are apt to be bad tempered and sometimes discourteous, but as lovers they are the most fascinating of men. They are usually able to attract any woman they want to, and if they marry according to their own desires, are the happiest type, as they are never drawn to any but women as ardent as themselves. The same is true of women with this type of handwriting.

THE PEOPLE IN BETWEEN

Between each of these types of handwriting—"Passionate," "Cold," and "Self-Centered"—there are several specific kinds that have not yet been fully discussed. These are the "in between" people.

The "Cold" type, you will remember—who has the upright handwriting—is the least emotional. These people are pleasant, kind, even-tempered, but unloving in the sense that they do not show emotion. Here is a person who will nurse you when you are sick, speak softly to you when you are in trouble, but it will never occur to him or her to caress you or press soft and deep kisses on your mouth. This person would think such things indelicate. When a very ardent man marries this type he is due for all kinds of disappointments, and when he is about 50, he is likely to kick up his heels in a way that will astonish his ladylike wife.

The next notch to the left of the upright position in handwriting is the same as "Cold," only more so. This person does not know that such a thing as a kiss exists, except to shudder with distaste when the thing is mentioned. This person may or may not be kind—but the only way he shows it is by paying attention sometimes, or ignoring you otherwise.

The second notch to the left is the secretly "passionate" type, which we have mentioned. They hide their emotions in public, express them in private.

The third notch to the left is the writing of the person who is all taken up with ideals of beauty which have nothing to do with people. He loves his home, his country, flowers, and poetry. He knows many things—but not much about people. A loving woman who marries this type may content herself with his fine character, but unless she is interested in the same things he is, she will often find herself alone. An ardent man who is married to this type woman, even though he may continue to love her, is apt to wander from her side.

If the writing is large, in this third notch to the left—or if it leans even further to the left—you have the ardent, demonstrative type, who is practically the same as the right-leaning type. He or she is a highly emotional person—who likes people—but is apt to get into arguments over petty things.

The first notch *to the right* of the upright position, is just a shade more demonstrative than the "Cold" type, and a bit more apt to have humor and love of pleasure in the character. These are ideal mothers and fathers. They love the hearth and children. Animals and plants thrive under their care. Such people lose active interest in each other after a few children are born—and continue, not as lover and sweetheart, but "mother" and "father." Men of this type will never stray, after about the age of 40.

If a man who is very ardent marries this "mildly passionate" type, he will never forget that he wants a sweetheart as well as a mother for his children. He may, indeed, stray—and his wife will never be able to see how she failed him.

The second notch to the right of the upright position is the normally loving person who is outgoing, gregarious, likes people, and tends to show it. These are the ones who like a caress and can give a thrilling one, and yet will not overdo it as will people whose writing slants rightward to the third, fourth, and fifth notch on the Love Meter.

* * * * * *

Writing that slants every which way—right, left, straight up and down—usually indicates great confusion. It means the person is undergoing some sort of crisis or is having trouble making up his or her mind about something. It may be a very personal matter that the person has been concealing from parents, husband, or wife—trying to decide who to confide in, or whether or not it should be kept secret.

EXCESSIVE LOVE INTEREST

Writing of this nature—that slants every which way—with two additional signs, indicates a very disturbed attitude in matters of love—excessive love interest. These signs, according

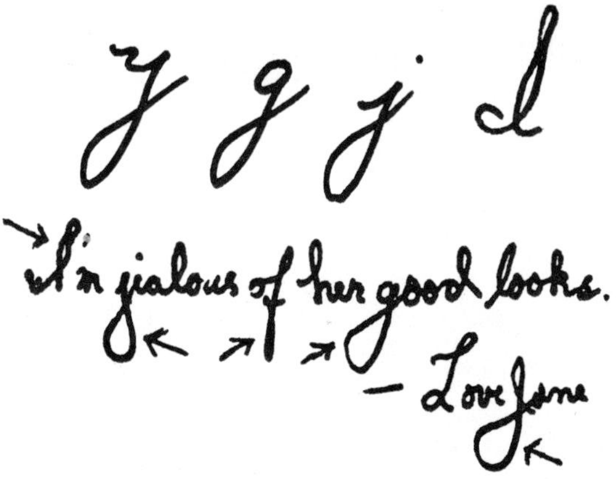

Fig. 6

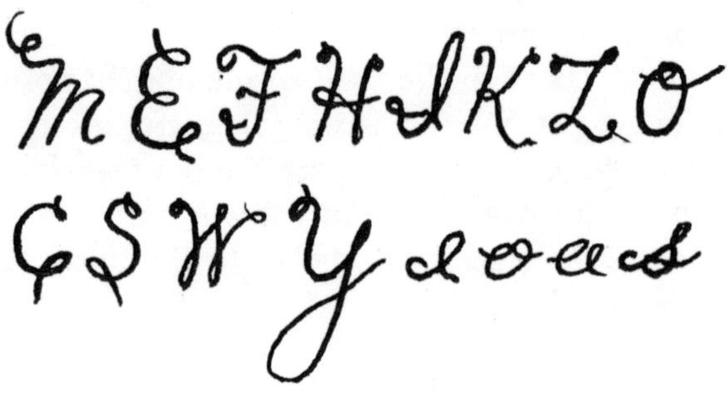

Fig. 7

to Hal Falcon, Ph.D.*, are: (1) excessively large lower loops in the letters *y, g,* and *j,* and (2) a capital *I* with a stricture in it (an indentation on both sides of the loop, forming a sort of narrow figure 8).† (See Fig. 6.)

When you see these signs in writing, he says, run—don't walk—to the nearest exit,and don't come back until the person is gone. People with this type of writing, he says, need professional help, which the average person is not equipped to give.

Other signs that indicate this frame of mind are excessive and unnecessary loops in the letters shown in Fig. 7.

Fig. 8

---

*Hal Falcon, *How to Analyze Handwriting* (New York, N.Y.: Cornerstone Library) 1964.

†This indicates a disturbed mental condition.

According to Dr. Falcon, lower-looped letters such as *g, j, p, y* show—with extreme accuracy—whether a person feels he is loved or unloved, and his or her wants, needs, and desires in this direction. The larger the loop, the greater the person's desire, he says. The smaller the loop—including incomplete loops on the letters *g* and *y*—the smaller the desire. (See Fig. 8.)

The length of these lower loops, he says, tells you the same thing. Normal interests and needs are shown by normal-sized lower loops, which are *equal* in size to the upper loops of the letters *b, d, f, h, k, l,* and *t*. These people have no more than normal love needs or desires.

Lack of interest is shown when most of the lower loops are shorter than the upper loops.

Above-average interest is shown when most of the lower loops are 10% or more, greater in length than the upper-looped letters.

The length of time a person feels it has been since he or she felt sexually or emotionally satisfied, is shown by the distance between the lower loop and the base line of writing.

If the loop comes right up to the base line of writing and crosses it, this indicates that the person feels he is being satisfied in love at present. This is typical of married people (Fig. 9).

If the loop does not come up to the base line of writing, but crosses further down, it means the person feels it's been a long

Fig. 9

$$g$$

Fig. 10

time since he felt satisfied, sexually or emotionally. This is typical for widows, divorcees, bachelors, and unmarried women (Fig. 10).

The further down the loop crosses—or if it doesn't cross at all (that is, if the lower loop is left incomplete)—the longer it's been, as far as the person is concerned. Loops that are uncrossed, or crossed far down near the end of the tail of *y, g,* and *j* show a complete lack of interest in these matters. This is typical of scholars, teachers, doctors, and clergymen, when they are deeply involved in their work.

WHO IS YOUR PERFECT MATE?

First of all, we must realize that very few of the marriages which are unhappy are so because of any real fault in either person. They are unhappy because of the early training each received in childhood—and their *response* to that training, habits which are very difficult to break.

If you grew up in a situation where it was best for you to remain calm, cool, and logical—let's say, this is the way your parents were—then you would be calm, cool, and logical, too.

If you grew up in a situation where nobody cared for you, then it was best for you to be self-centered—to look out for yourself, thinking always, "What's best for me?" And no matter how successful you became, you would always feel a little insecure.

If you grew up in a situation where everyone was affectionate, good-humored, generous, and cared for everyone else, you too would inherit much of this "Passionate" nature. It would be in your nature to share, without feeling hurt, cheated, resentful, or sorry for yourself.

How does this apply to the Love Meter? How does it answer the question: Who is your perfect mate?

To begin with, it is quite obvious that a "cool" person using the upright handwriting, with plain, rounded letter formations, will never make a person happy in marriage whose writing leans far to the right, and who has extreme excitability, love of pleasure, and intense emotionalism as the basis of his character.

Generally speaking, the safe thing for the person with upright handwriting to do is marry another whose writing is of the upright type.

A forward-leaning writer should marry another whose handwriting is also forward-leaning (to the right). Each of these "Passionate" people will usually try to give twice as much as he or she receives—and such a marriage may well last a lifetime.

The backhand writer (slanting left), with small, meek, and precise letter formations, can marry safely with the upright handwriter, or the almost upright hand. The uncertainty of the backhand writer will find safety and security in a mate of the upright letter type, whose mind is calm and logical. Both are good planners with a similar outlook on life and little show of outward emotion.

The backhand writer with wild, irregular letter formations can marry a forward-leaning writer with a fair promise of happiness, since—while the forward leaner is very affectionate and outgoing—the large, scrawling backhand writer is, also, basically affectionate (although with a tendency to be self-conscious and take offense at petty things).

Remember that the pressure of the man's writing should be about twice as heavy as the woman's, because if his is only equal to hers, or lighter, then on some occasions he will react to a situation in a way that she is bound to consider weak or namby-pamby. And she will not respect him.

If there could be a ticket pinned to every man and woman giving the exact degree of affection which is in their makeup, about two-thirds of the divorce cases would disappear from the court calendar. And there *is* such a way—through handwriting—according to graphologists.

Mildly loving, passionately loving, jealously loving, totally unloving—if you will look at the Love Meter on page 148, you will see that all these can be easily recognized by anyone.

IF MOOD CHANGES—WRITING CHANGES

Many people insist that they have two types of writing—sometimes to the right, sometimes to the left, sometimes large, sometimes small, sometimes straight up and down. And so they well may. *But the rule still holds.* Whatever traits you show in ordinary, everyday living show up in your handwriting. If your handwriting changes, it's because your mood changes. And there are certain traits in handwriting that never change, no matter how hard you may try to disguise your writing. These show up mostly in your lower letters—some of which we have already examined, and others we will see shortly.

The important point to remember, psychologists say, is that no person is 100 percent good or bad. No person is 100 per cent selfish or generous. No person is 100 per cent cold or passionate. Every person is a complicated mixture of these things, and all that psychologists—or anybody else—can do, is point out which emotions are expressed most frequently.

IS HE OR SHE IN A GOOD
OR BAD MOOD?

The method by which a person's mood can be discovered in handwriting is simplicity itself. The rule is: uphill means a good mood, downhill means a bad one. Let me quote Sonnemann* at this point:

"Indications of feeling of optimism, zeal, 'elevation,' suggest themselves for rising lines. . . . The line 'falls' whenever the arm of the person . . . gradually sinks back toward the body . . . and

---

*Ulrich Sonnemann, Ph.D., *Handwriting Analysis as a Diagnostic Tool* (New York, N.Y.: Grune & Stratton, 1950).

its psychological correlate, discouragement or depression, will suggest itself."

He also suggests that slight downhill lines occurring after several pages "is simply the common consequence of normal muscular fatigue; and that straight lines—even with the bottom of the page—indicate an even temperament, not easily influenced by good or bad moods."

Let me add that, not only have I found these observations to be true, in case after case, but I have also found some relation between downhill writing and poor health.

WHAT THIS "SECRET WINDOW" TELLS
YOU ABOUT PERFECT STRANGERS

At this point, let me give you a few examples of what handwriting can reveal about total strangers—people you have never even seen before. When I first became interested in handwriting, I read so many books and became so enthusiastic about it, that others began to get curious, too, as to just what information this "secret window" could reveal.

Strange as it may seem, I began getting many requests from friends and acquaintances to analyze their writing—but they were *anonymous* requests, signed with false names and passed along to me by a mutual acquaintance, who refused to tell me the real identities of the writers. But in case after case, the writer eventually came forward, to let me know just how accurate I was.

I wish to emphasize that at no time—except in one case— had I ever seen the handwriting of the person before. I had no idea whose handwriting I was looking at. Yet, in case after case, I was astounded at the accuracy of what this "secret window" revealed—as were the people themselves, who were occasionally quite embarrassed, but admitted the truth of what I saw.

REVEALS "SECRET MARRIAGE"

The very first time I tried this method, an astounding revelation came to light—which, one month later, proved to be true. I received a sample of the handwriting of a person named "Eileen."

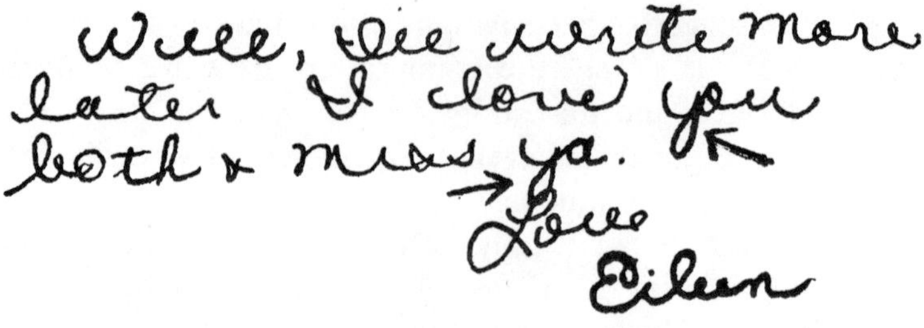

Fig. 11

The woman who gave it to me said it was her daughter, whom I had never met. Here is what I wrote:

> Dear Mrs. G.—
>
> Since your daughter's handwriting slants to the right, it means she is outgoing and gregarious. Since some of the letters are almost upright, it means she is good with figures and money.
>
> Yet since many others slant to the far right, she enjoys meeting people, has good managerial potential, inspires confidence among her peers, and is a natural leader.
>
> Since the smaller letters tend to slant every which way, it means she is having trouble making up her mind about something. A lot of trouble.
>
> Pen pressure is fairly strong. It means she has drive, energy, and enthusiasm. The base line of writing is straight —as though there were lines on the paper—and this shows good coordination and rhythm. She's physically agile, should be good at sports, good with her hands (could learn to play music, for example).
>
> One's love life is revealed, in all cases, in all people, by the lower-case letters *j, q, p, g, y.* If the lower loop comes up to the base line of writing and crosses it, it indicates that one is satisfied as far as this is concerned. Eileen's comes right up and crosses in every case.

There was more, but these were the important parts of the letter. Eileen *was* outgoing. She *was* popular. She *was* a natural leader. In fact, she was *president* of the student government at the college she was attending. She *was* good with numbers. In fact, she was studying to become a high school math teacher when she graduated. She was a student athlete and an excellent piano player. She belonged to many clubs.

The surprising part was that she did not show the typical writing of a single girl—the loops should have been crossed further down from the line of writing—and she *was* single, supposedly. Her writing showed no excessive love interest (the lower loops were no longer than the upper ones). But she did show confusion—letters slanting every which way—trouble making up her mind about something.

This analysis was done in February of 1967. In March, it was discovered she had already been married for three months, but had been afraid to tell her mother because she feared her husband would not meet her parent's high expectations (he was not wealthy).

It is interesting to note that this is not the only case of such a revelation in my experience. Several times I have detected such situations in handwriting—and the people involved have admitted that they were true.

REVEALS "PASSIONATE" NATURE

In another case, I received a mysterious note from a woman, asking me to analyze her handwriting. It was signed, "Trananda Waltmiller," and was handed to me by a friend, who refused to reveal the writer's identity.

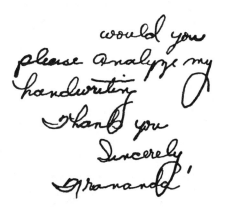

Fig. 12

As you can see, it was just a short note, but from this brief sample, I was able to see many things. *And all of the traits* which I noticed from this small sample, appeared again—magnified a thousand times—in her "Thank you" note to me.

Here is what I wrote to "Trananda":

> Dear Trananda:
>
> You are not bashful. In fact you have a forceful personality. You could manage people and be successful in any field involving selling, because your enthusiasm for the product would be contagious. But you prefer not to.
>
> You have drive, enthusiasm, aggressiveness, and you're a good socializer. You are exceedingly curious about things, and often follow that curiosity with fanatical zeal.
>
> Justice is as important to you as truth, and if you found, for example, that someone was "getting away" with something unjustly, and to the disadvantage of others, you'd speak up about it right away and prove your point.
>
> You are of a passionate nature and have very strong desires. You are either not married, separated from your husband or boyfriend, or just not. It is possible that you have many boyfriends, since your passionate nature makes you attractive to men. Yet subconsciously you feel it's been a long time since you were satisfied.
>
> You tend to become tired physically rather than mentally. This may be caused by overeating.
>
> Your passionate nature plays a great part in your personality. It seeks outlets. It makes you generous. It makes you care for other people. And together with your intelligence, it gives you a great sense of humor.

There was more, of course. But "Trananda" turned out to be one of the most popular girls I knew. I had never seen her writing before, and I was surprised to find out just how warm a person she was. This is revealed by the excessive number of loops in almost all of her letters, the extreme length of her *y*'s, *g*'s, and *f*'s, the extreme size of the lower loops (it is a fact, for example, that Marilyn Monroe had an enormous lower loop in her signature, as well as an excessive number of loops in her other letters), and the rightward slant of her writing. "Trananda" was not married at the time, which was also revealed in her writing. One thing which I did not mention in my analysis was the her handwriting showed a bit of a sadistic streak, revealed in some of her lower-looped letters, which were cut off extremely short.

REVEALS "COLD" PERSONALITY

I received another anonymous note, signed "Jane Harris," which—surprisingly enough—turned out to be the initials of her real name. I did not realize this at the time, though.

Even though this handwriting slants to the right, it is basically "cold" because it is almost upright. This is the typical handwriting of a person who is extremely self-conscious, though not necessarily selfish. (Note the slow, careful writing and the extremely "dramatic" way she dots the *i*'s and exclamation points.) Here was what I told her:

> This person is interested in people. She can be very expressive and enjoys good conversation. She should never play poker, because what she feels is often written all over her face.
>
> She has a flair for the dramatic, likes people to be impressed with her, tends to exaggerate a little. She's a pretty good actress; what she says is often not what she feels.

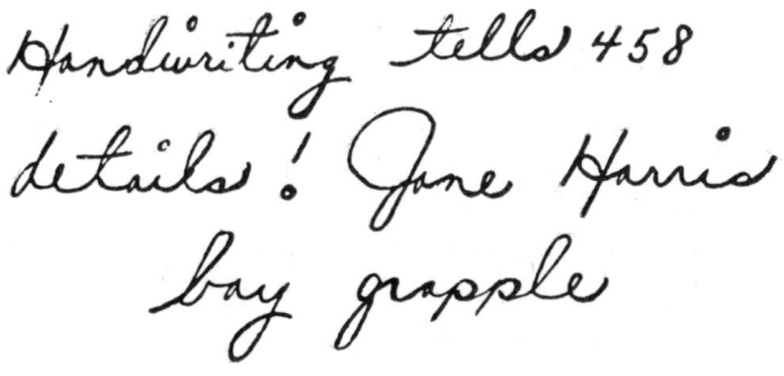

Fig. 13

She has a sadistic streak; often enjoys making other people squirm.

She's a slow, deliberate person in all her actions. She thinks a good deal about what she says before she says it. She has a tendency to put things off.

She's good with figures, can handle her money, and is a good planner. She has manual dexterity (she's good with her hands), could learn to operate any machine easily, may even have an artistic flair.

Either she has no more than normal interest in men or does not demonstrate such interest outwardly. She can be very responsive, if she wants to. She feels, subconsciously at least, that it has been a long time since she has been satisfied. Either not married, separated from husband or boyfriend, or just not emotionally involved at this time.

This is the typical handwriting of a single person, with a space between where the lower loop crosses and the line of writing. It will be a long time before this particular girl marries—if she marries at all—because of her cold, self-centered, and sadistic streaks. And if she does get married—unless it is to someone with an upright or left-leaning handwriting—the marriage is not likely to be a happy one. (In other words, if she marries a person whose writing slants more to the right than hers, he is apt to be disappointed in her lack of responsiveness.) As was mentioned before, the sadistic streak is noted by the two *p*'s, which are cut short.

LEFT SIDE	RIGHT SIDE
HEAD NECK CHEST	
WAIST ABDOMEN	
CROTCH THIGHS LEGS ANKLES, FEET	

Fig. 14

HEALTH SIGNS IN WRITING

In writing, your mind unconsciously treats all letters of the alphabet as if they represented the human body, as Figure 14 shows.

Thus, in case after case, it has been shown that any indentation, revealed in the majority of letters on the same side in the same place corresponds to a physical debility of some kind.

This can also be revealed by an abnormally thick spot in a line that should be smooth, or a gap in a line that should not be broken.

Note: *You will never get a completely true reading from a sample done with a ball-point pen, since ball-point pens have been known to skip, and make ink blots (and even the best of them skip on smooth paper). For this reason, handwriting experts always try to avoid samples done with ball-point pens, preferring a sharp #2 pencil instead, on regular white unlined paper—with a backing of several sheets of paper underneath, if possible (although you can't always be choosy about the samples you get). A fountain pen may be used if it is of good quality.**

Here are a few examples of health indications in writing.

Fig. 14—A

---

*It is interesting, also, to note that the type of writing instrument a person habitually uses, indicates much about his personality. If he uses a hard-point #3 pencil that makes thin, weak lines, he is generally of a quiet, soft-spoken nature. If he uses thick, felt-tipped pens (called markers) most of the time, you may be sure he has a more forceful, dynamic personality —more so than average—the kind of personality that wants to be noticed.

1. CHEST TROUBLE Here is an indentation on the letter *b*, on the right
   side of the loop, near the middle. (See Fig. 14-A.) On the chart in
   Figure 14, you can see that this is in the vicinity of the chest, on the
   right side.

Fig. 14-B

Fig. 14-C

gelatin book

Fig. 14-D

2. LEG TROUBLE Here we see a space skipped on the loop in the letter *y*, on the right side. This means an injury or weakness in the person's right leg, although he may not be aware of it yet. (See Fig. 14-B.)

3. HEAD WOUND An indentation on the top of a loop means a head injury of some sort. This one is on the right side of the letter *l*. It could be the head or right ear. (See Fig. 14-C.)

4. HEART TROUBLE Heart trouble may be indicated by any indentation, light spot, or thickening, in the area of the chest, on Figure 14, on the right side. (See Fig. 14-D.)

Now we come to several body signs for which the chart in Figure 14 is not needed. The meaning of these signs has been determined by experts, over a period of 50 years, from thousands of sample handwritings tested.

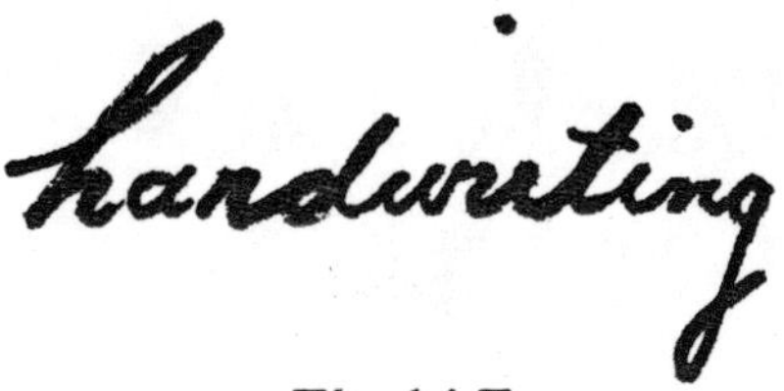

Fig. 14-E

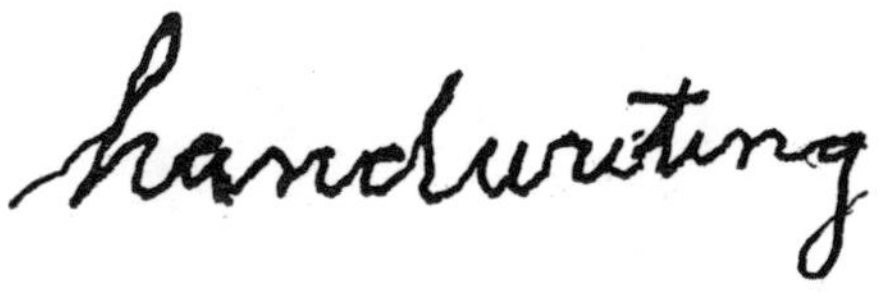

Fig. 14-F

5. FATIGUE Uneven, heavy and light pressure has been found to indicate one thing: fatigue. There may be a number of reasons for this, from heart trouble, emphysema, or diabetes to low blood sugar. Or it may be due to simple exhaustion from overworking. It may also result from overeating, especially in people with a right slant. (See Fig. 14-E.)

6. STAMMERING Stuttering or stammering are caused by muscular spasms that force the repetition of sounds. This shows up in handwriting as repeated lines or wavering lines. Retracing of lines has also been found to be a sign of lying or dishonesty. (See Fig. 14-F.)

7. CORONARY SPASMS OR STROKE You can tell this from the awkward, angular shape of many of the letters, and a wavering quality in other letters, as though it had been written with the wrong hand (as indeed many stroke victims are forced to do). (See Fig. 14-G.)

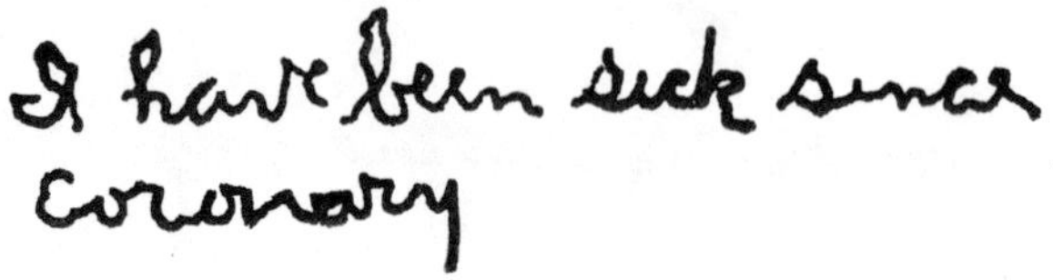

I have been sick since Coronary

Fig. 14-G

handwriting

Fig. 14-H

8. ARTHRITIS The handwriting of an arthritic person, with painful, swollen joints, is similar to #7 in slight awkwardness, and occasional irregularities, such as sharp points instead of curves. But it is much clearer than #7. (See Fig. 14-H.)

You should never play "doctor" or frighten the person whose handwriting you are reading. Instead, you should tell him that you are not perfect, but urge him to have a medical examination as soon as possible—if his handwriting shows some evidence of physical disability.

DISHONESTY OR INSINCERITY

The unnecessary retracing of lines has been found to be a sign of lying, insincerity, or the withholding of information. (See Figure 14-I.)

Figure 14-I also shows one of the classic signs of dishonesty: many of the letters are completely open or disconnected at the base, having been written with at least two strokes.

THE VAIN PERSON

It has been found that two of the signs of vanity in handwriting are the incomplete lower loop on the y, forming a "V" shape (Fig. 14-J), and circles instead of dots on i's and exclamation points (Fig. 13).

Fig. 14-I

Fig. 14-J

Such people can easily be flattered and tend to have a flair for the dramatic, exaggerating all their troubles in an attempt to elicit sympathy from others.

THE SADISTIC PERSON

It has been found that letters with lower loops that are cut short are often the sign of a sadistic streak in the writer. (See Fig. 12.)

This type of person derives enjoyment from watching others squirm. He likes to embarrass people, just to see them suffer. He is often a prankster or practical joker. Note the heavy down-stroke in all his letters. (See Fig. 14-K.)

Fig. 14-K

Fig. 14-L

MALE AND FEMALE SYMBOLS

It has been found time and again that the loop or abnormally long line is the male symbol in writing, and that the person who shows an excessive number of these is thinking about men, or sex. (See Fig. 14-L.)

The triangle in lower-looped letters has come to be known as the female symbol. (See Fig. 14—M.)

If a woman shows many triangles in her handwriting, it can mean that she's an actress, dress designer, ballet dancer, model— and that, for this reason, the female body is on her mind a lot. Similarly, if a man's writing shows an excessive number of loops, it may mean that his living depends upon keeping his

Fig. 14-M

body in shape. He may be a laborer, athlete, coach, or men's clothing designer.

REVEALS HIS "SECRET DESIRE"

Linda J. was very much in love with a man she had met at a church social. He was polite—but seemingly "cold" toward her—and she couldn't help but wonder why. She had heard about this method of finding out what's on people's minds, through a friend, and managed to get a sample of his handwriting. From this "secret window," she immediately saw that he was either not married, separated from his wife or girlfriend, or just not emotionally involved with anyone at the present time. She also learned that—although he seemed cold on the outside—he was really a "secretly passionate" person who liked girls, but was just shy.

Once she learned these facts, Linda was much more confident and sure of herself. The next time they met, she simply struck up a conversation with him and found—to her amazement—that he really *was* warm and friendly, that he was single, and that he was very attracted to her. Their friendship deepened, and today both are happily married.

SEES WHAT BOYFRIEND IS REALLY DOING

Polly V. was engaged to a man who had borrowed a great deal of money from her and proposed marriage. On one of his frequent "business" trips, he made the mistake of writing to her, however. And from this small sample of his writing—like a "secret window" into his mind—she was able to see, immediately, what he was really doing. In the first place, his handwriting showed that he was probably already married, or going with someone else with whom he was deeply involved.

In the second place, it showed marked signs of lying, dishonesty, and the withholding of facts. Panic-stricken, Polly immediately had him investigated and found all this—and more—to be true.

Never again was this man able to fool her or take advantage of her. Today, happily married to someone good and true, she was able to avoid a lifetime of trouble and heartache with this simple method.

REVEALS FORTUNE-MAKING OPPORTUNITY

Larry M. was stuck in a job he didn't like, barely earning enough to make ends meet. Furthermore, he saw no future with the Post Office Department, but he hadn't the slightest idea what to do to get out of his rut and into a higher-paying job. He came to me, seeking advice, complaining that he had a wife and child to support, plus car and mortgage payments, and that he couldn't do it on $80 a week. I showed him how to look into the "secret window" of his handwriting.

Both of us immediately saw that he had a natural gift for selling, and getting along with people. He was a natural-born leader, fun-loving, and outgoing. I advised him to get into any line of work where he could use his ability to get along with people. Larry took this advice and became a salesman for a large department store.

Soon he began receiving pay raises, bonuses, and of course, thousands of dollars in commissions. Today he is in charge of many people, making $15,000 a year—plus stock options and profit sharing totaling $3,000 a year more, tax-free, without a lick of extra work.

He has two cars, a split-level home in the suburbs, with beautiful furniture, all the modern conveniences, and six weeks a year paid vacations to enjoy it. He is happier than he's ever been, in a job that seems more like play—all thanks to the simple secret revealed in these pages.

"SECRET WINDOW" REVEALS DANGER— SAVES FATHER'S LIFE

Now that she was married, Elizabeth E. rarely had a chance to see her father, Warren E., 60, who lived several hundred miles away, in a different state. But they wrote to each other often, and one day, from the "secret window" of her father's writing, Elizabeth noticed some kind of injury or weakness in the vicinity of his chest. She immediately wrote to him, and informed him of this, urging him to see a doctor and get it checked.

Several weeks later, a letter arrived from her father, in which he expressed amazement at what she had been able to see so accurately. It was true, he said, that he hadn't been feeling too well, but he hadn't wanted to worry her. When he received her letter, however, he decided to get it checked, and discovered—from EKG tests that the doctor had given him—that he did, indeed, have a slight heart condition, which, if he had let it go, might have developed into something serious.

Thanks to this method, he was helped in time, and now he felt fit, healthy, and invigorated—completely free of pain.

CHECKLIST OF THINGS TO LOOK FOR THROUGH YOUR "SECRET WINDOW"

* Small writing is an indication of the possession of concentration; the ability to accomplish a great deal with the least expenditure of effort.

* Large handwriting—flowing, gracious, and written with ease—shows facility in talking, graciousness of manner, and usually the ability to adapt oneself to different surroundings.

* Wide margins indicate the possession of good taste and usually the desire to spend money.

* Light pressure of the pen reflects refinement in taste and temperament, a controlled temper, but an unfortunate tendency toward laziness and putting things off.

* Heavy pressure, as a rule, shows good health, a love of pleasure, great energy, and enthusiasm. Successful businessmen generally use heavy pressure.

* Sloppy, unclean writing is often the result of rapid writing, in which the pen is desperately trying to overtake the racing thoughts. Clear writing is often the result of slower but more accurate thinking.

* Large capitals show pride and a desire for achievement.

* When the signature is in backhand and the body of the writing leans forward, the writer appears cold and unfriendly but is the reverse.

* A forward-leaning signature with the body of the writing backward is the indication of a personality which seems far more ardent and loving than the character really is.

* A straight line beneath the signature is the indication of a forceful personality, which is less tactful and gracious than it might be.
* Curved underscores to signatures show grace of manner, adaptability, and the capacity for influencing others.
* The underscore which consists of one or two almost straight lines, in the middle of which are two short perpendicular lines, is the sign of commercial instincts.
* A curved or wavy line *over* the signature is hardly ever seen, but is the expression of a very eccentric and very odd personality. These people are sometimes so odd as to seem a bit unbalanced.

The reasons why people have their handwritings (or the handwritings of others) analyzed are many and varied. Some people are shocked, upon looking through this "secret window" to see that a person is not what he seems to be. A man may meet a girl and want to know more about her before he asks her for a date. Or the girl may want to know more about the boy. Parents may want to know about their children. Wives and husbands may want to know more about each other—in an effort to strengthen and unite all family ties.

Handwriting can tell you all these things, and more, for it is a secret window into the human mind.

Psycho-Command Power #8

HOW TO GET SOMETHING
FOR NOTHING!

In ancient times, money was reported to have been obtained by the use of magic spells. So-called Druid stones were claimed to bring riches. In Africa, the giving of money to the spirit Zebus from the Kingdom of Uranus was said to double it. In ancient Greece, the amount desired was written on a piece of parchment and placed within the hollow of a wax figure of the goddess Hecate, which was then burned upon an altar. The methods were often elaborate.

> In a book called *Magical Ritual* (n.d.) by "Eliphas Lévi" (also known as Alphonse Louis Constant)—the last of the great sorcerers—there are instructions for the formation and consecration of a Magic Wand, reportedly able to bring one's desires.

It was made of the wood of a newly matured nut or almond tree, cut off with one blow of a sickle, a hollow tube bored through it, end to end (without any cracks), and a magnetized steel needle, the same length, inserted. One end was sealed with a clear glass bead, the other with resin, and both ends covered with sachets of silk. One copper and one zinc ring were affixed to the center, and two lengths of fine copper chain wound around the wand. On it were written the names of the Twelve Spirits of the Zodiac, with their sigils: Aries/Sarahiel, Taurus/Araziel, Gemini/Saraiel, Cancer/Phakiel, Leo/Seratiel, Virgo/Schaltiel, Libra/Chadakiel, Scorpio/Sartziel, Sagittarius/Saritiel, Capricornus/Semaquiel, Aquarius/Tzakmaquel, Pisces/Vacabiel. Upon the copper ring were engraved in Hebrew letters, from right to left, the words, "The Holy Jerusalem," H QDshH JRUshLIM; and upon the zinc ring in Hebrew letters, from right to left, the words "The King Solomon," H MLK shLMH, Heh Melek Shelomoh. It was consecrated by the invocation of the Spirits of the Four Elements and the Seven Planets, by ceremonies lasting seven days, using special incense and prayers for each day. It was kept wrapped in silk and never allowed in contact with any color but black.

*   *   *   *   *   *

Was all this necessary, however? Is there a simpler way? A way to get something for nothing? The answer to these last two questions is "Yes, there is!" And the explanation is quite reasonable.

> **Everything you get in life, you get in exchange for an invisible object—an idea, goal, or thought within your mind. Real objects, in the outer world, are only symbols of these ideas. Riches, treasures, luxuries—the things you get from others—are only their *ideas* (in physical form) of how they can repay you for kindnesses.**

Here, in this chapter, you'll discover how to get what you want from people—not with money, but through "psychic power control." In other words, you'll discover how to "get something for nothing"—literally, actually!

A MAGIC SPELL THAT WORKS LIVING MIRACLES

Suppose I were to give you a pouch full of golden powder, magic powder that you could sprinkle in the air that would instantly bring you whatever you desired.

> Just a pinch of this powder, sprinkled in the air, would instantly make any man or woman do your bidding, without even realizing that they were under a magic spell. Just a pinch of this powder would make others like you, defer to you, and want to please you wherever you go.

What would you give for such a magic powder? A hundred? A thousand? A million dollars? Would it surprise you to know that there *is* such a charm—and that it is free—although different than you may have imagined!

THE MAGIC MIRROR TECHNIQUE FOR GETTING YOUR WAY WITH OTHERS

There is a technique for getting your way with others, which I call the Magic Mirror Technique. Like all the techniques in this book, it depends upon the power of suggestion upon the human mind.

The Magic Mirror Technique is a million times more powerful—and a million times easier—than even hypnosis. It consists, simply, of *telling people what they want to hear*, of allowing them to see just what they want to see, or appearing to do for them just what they want or feel needs to be—or should be—done.

> It is exactly like flashing a Magic Mirror in the eyes of those you wish to influence—or using a real magic wand. By telling them what they want to hear, or doing what they feel ought to be done, it is possible to "plant" ideas in the minds of others—the idea that you are the good and worthy person they always hoped existed, the idea that your kindness must be repaid in some way, the idea that you are deserving of some gift, some favor, some reward.

Often, the Magic Mirror Technique requires little more than good manners—like smiling or appearing intensely interested in someone's conversation.

Take the matter of intelligent listening in conversation, for example. Simply by *listening*—without uttering a sound or lifting one little finger—you can make yourself admired and respected, so that others look upon you as "aces high."

If you can listen without impatience to talkative individuals —and be a good listener, even to the most trivial details—they will think you are truly an intelligent person, simply because you have not disagreed with them and have listened patiently. Even those of a violent nature will be calmed by your soothing attitude and personality.

Avoid arguments on any and all subjects, and you will make friends by seeming to agree with people.

There is nothing dishonest about this. On the contrary, you are actually *helping* the person to whom you are quietly listening, by giving him a chance to vent his emotions, get all or most of what's bothering him "off his chest." This makes him a calmer, easier person to get along with. Even if he is wrong, the mere act of allowing him to speak at length, examining the matter from all sides, will often—and almost invariably—lead him to realize the error of his ways.

The silent suggestions which you make, using this secret—compelling the other person to like you, admire you, want to do favors for you—may or may not be true.

But if the person upon whom you have used the Magic Mirror believes them to be true, believes that you like or admire or agree with him, he is in a state of hypnosis, and you have made him think as you wish.

Any person who thinks as you wish will soon do as you wish. The law is absolute and your rewards are guaranteed.

HOW THIS SECRET CAN BRING YOU
ANYTHING YOU DESIRE

The power of suggestion upon the human mind may be likened unto a seed which, when dropped upon fertile soil, has the power to grow, take root, and assume form.

It is exactly like sprinkling a Magic Powder of Enchantment in the air that draws your desires to you. Your thoughts and desires actually transmit themselves to those around you. They reach out, imposing themselves, and others accept them as having originated in themselves, as the expression of their own desires, their own intention.

So powerful is the force of suggestion upon others that you have merely to "plant" these suggestions—like sprinkling seeds—then jump back and watch them blossom into reality.

Now let us see how this secret may be used to bring your desires to you easily and automatically!

RECEIVES FUR COAT

For years, Martha D. had longed for the day when she could have her own fur coat. But for years, she knew that her husband could not afford such a luxury, and so she wore the same inexpensive cloth coats she had always worn. Finally, the time arrived when, with the children grown, Martha was sure it would no longer be a hardship.

At first, she tried subtle hints, like mentioning that some friend had just bought a lovely new fur coat. There was no response from her husband. Then she tried to impress him with the fact that she had been wearing the same old "rags" for years, and that the fur coats pictured in the newspaper ads were really very good buys. Apparently, her husband was not impressed.

Finally, in desperation, she took to scolding and berating him for ignoring her, for spending money on himself, but never on her. She would plead, and beg, and throw temper tantrums at every opportunity, reminding him of all the sacrifices she had made over the years. All to no avail.

For a long time, Martha sulked and felt sorry for herself, and refused to talk to her husband. She sulked for such a long time, that eventually she overcame her initial shock and outrage at her husband's refusal to buy her a coat. She began to think about the matter in a clear, calm, logical manner. Here was her plan.

He would have to buy her the coat because *he* wanted to, she reasoned. He would have to think it was *his* idea, and she would have to "plant" this desire in his mind. Using the Magic Mirror Technique, she decided to do things for him that she hadn't done in years.

She would treat him special and show him that now that the children were grown, *he* was the one who really mattered, *he* was the most important individual in the household, all-wise, all-powerful, all-deserving. She would shower him with love and attention, make him contented in every way, and, without saying a word, make him even feel a little ashamed that he was receiving so much from her and giving so little in return.

She would do this until he forgot about the fur coat. Then, having built up his confidence, she would find a way to shake him up a little—without being obvious, without asking for the coat. She would wait until one of her friends received the gift of a new item of apparel, such as a dress or a new coat, and she would immediately invite this couple to dinner, perhaps for a game of cards, so her friend—or her friend's husband—could brag about it. This, she knew, would embarrass him—enough, she hoped, so that he would actually offer to buy her a new coat.

And this strategy, repeated several times, on several dinner occasions, actually did begin to have its effect on her husband. He began to make noises about her clothes, urging her to dress up more, fix her hair. He never suggested anything as expensive as a fur coat, but give him time, she knew, and he would work himself up to it. And sure enough, he did.

But he did it in his own way, almost casually, so as not to make himself look foolish, but rather suddenly generous, as though he were giving in. It was on an ordinary shopping day, while they were strolling through the Women's Garment section of a department store, that he stopped to look at the fur coats.

"You know, you ought to try one of these on," he said. "I think it's about time we showed our friends a thing or two."

Seconds later Martha was wearing a new silver fox fur coat. She hugged it to her bosom. It was hers, she knew. And what all her years of begging and pleading had failed to do, the Magic Mirror had finally accomplished—automatically!

RECEIVES GIFT OF GLITTERING JEWELS

Jill was just so happy that her boyfriend was home from Vietnam that she had no wants, no desires, other than to make him happy, too. There was just one small problem, however. John had plans, so many plans, in fact, that he just never stopped talking about them. But none of these plans seemed to include marriage. What with going back to school and working to make ends meet, it seemed there just wouldn't be enough time or money to get married and start a family—at least not now.

This upset Jill greatly. She would work, she told him. That would help. And she would willingly sacrifice luxuries. She was sure they would be able to make a go of it.

John brushed all this aside, however, saying that in the long run it would be better to wait. And so, wherever they went, whenever John began talking excitedly about his plans, Jill just listened patiently, hoping that he would change his mind.

Meanwhile, John became greatly impressed with Jill's patience and understanding (this was Jill's *plan*), and his respect for her increased a thousandfold. He actually came to believe that she agreed with him, and her reliance upon his judgement pleased him.

He got a job after school hours, and he would go over to Jill's house, where she would fix something for him to eat and also help him study by quizzing him on what he was reading. Jill made herself so indispensable, in fact, that John began to feel deeply indebted to her.

Finally, to show his gratitude to her, John decided that he too would make a sacrifice of some sort. And with his savings, he bought Jill a beautiful diamond engagement ring, a lovely set of earrings, and a matching necklace.

After dinner and dancing at the best restaurant he could find, he presented these gifts to her. Quietly, John announced that he had just been offered a very good job, and after graduation, he would be honored if she would be his wife.

Jill immediately accepted—and once again, the Magic Mirror—whose strength and power is based on mutual respect and admiration—had worked its miracles.

RECEIVES FREE WARDROBE

Kathy and Jane were roommates, sharing an apartment in New York. Both were secretaries, and both were young and single. They were great chums and enjoyed taking turns cooking, playing the guitar and listening to records in the evening, and inviting guests over for dinner. Kathy enjoyed being a secretary, and she also had a boyfriend whom she frequently dated.

Jane was not quite as happy with the big city life, and being a secretary was a bit of a bore as far as she was concerned. Since she was single and unattached, Jane was seriously considering going into another line of work—one where the challenge would be greater, and where she would have more of an opportunity to help people, which she felt was the only thing really worthwhile. She was thinking of studying to be a dental assistant.

Kathy thought that this was a wonderful idea. But Jane soon pointed out that there was a small problem of money. She just couldn't see how she could manage to pay for schooling and also her full share of the apartment expenses.

Kathy told her not to worry, to go right ahead with her plan, as she would be more than glad to shoulder a few additional small expenses. After much hesitation and a firm promise to repay Kathy as soon as she was able, Jane enrolled in a course in dental hygiene.

Finally the day came when Jane became a licensed dental hygienist. And new excitement filled the girls' apartment as Jane explained to Kathy the wonderful opportunities there were for trained dental assistants with the WACs. Jane was still as determined as ever to repay Kathy for all her kindnesses. It bothered her that she was not able to give her a nice gift now, before she left—since she was still not earning any money. Jane thought and thought about it, but could not come up with any ideas—until, on the eve of her departure, it finally dawned on her. In the WACs, she would actually have no need of her civilian clothes. And she had a beautiful wardrobe, filled with the latest style dresses, suits, coats, pocketbooks, slacks, and shoes, many of them brand-new or hardly ever worn.

And so Jane decided to make a gift of her entire wardrobe to Kathy, as a "wedding present," for Kathy was soon to get married.

But Kathy's kindness was still not fully repaid, and, true to her word, several months after she had been in the WACs, Jane sent her a belated wedding gift of a $500 Savings Bond.

THEY RECEIVE A HOUSEFUL
OF NEW FURNITURE

When Larry and Marge G. moved into their new home in the suburbs, they were amazed at how friendly the neighbors were. In sharp contrast to the city, where they lived in the same apartment building with hundreds of other families and never knew many of them, this new environment was like a dream come true.

They were very anxious to meet and make friends with their new neighbors. Consequently, their neighbors returned this courtesy, and many of them went out of their way to meet and make friends with Marge and Larry. Time after time, these neighbors would introduce themselves, invite Larry and Marge into their homes, and show them around.

Marge became particularly good friends with her next door neighbor, Mrs. D. Mrs. D. worked, and Marge would occasionally babysit for her or receive large deliveries.

Suddenly—out of a clear blue sky—Mrs. D. told Marge that a relative of hers had recently died, leaving his house and all its furnishings to Mrs. D. and her husband. Mrs. D. had no use for the furniture and was planning to put an ad in the paper to try to sell it, or failing that, auction it off. But if Marge needed anything in the way of furniture, she would be perfectly welcome to look it over and take what she wanted, free.

Marge protested that she and Larry would be more than happy to pay for it, but Mrs. D. insisted that it was her present to Marge and Larry for being such good neighbors.

Larry and Marge paid a visit to the empty house and discovered that much of the furniture was either new or in very good condition. They were immediately attracted to a lovely living room and dining room set, with a large double sofa, tea table, end tables, lamps, and wing chairs. The master bedroom was also beautifully furnished, and Larry and Marge just couldn't make up their minds which to choose.

Mrs. D. solved the problem for them by giving them both sets of furniture—free!

HOW TO GET SOMETHING FOR NOTHING

When you use the Magic Mirror Technique, suddenly people will find themselves the victims of a strange compulsion to cooperate with and obey you—and they won't even know what's happening. They will never suspect that it is you who are impelling them to like you, please you, do favors for you, call you up and invite you to their homes, or visit you. People will seek you out, shake your hand, introduce themselves—and actually go out of their way to please you.

ASK FOR ANYTHING

Suppose there was a secret organization, with a secret telephone number that you could dial any time you wanted or needed something.

A member of this secret group would answer, take your request, and through secret ways—known only to members of this group—immediately see that you received whatever it was you asked for.

If, for example, you wanted money, you would simply dial this number, and members of this organization would see that you received any amount you needed—without cost or obligation.

If you felt you needed more love or companionship in your life, you'd simply dial this number, make your request, and the members of this group would see to it that a love interest would enter your life soon—perhaps several of them. Or maybe a host of new friends, if that's what you asked for . . .

You might desire a way to break through social barriers . . . contact a long-lost friend or relative . . . there would be no limit to the things you could receive. If you wanted new friends, secret knowledge, a spiritual healing, or anything else, you'd simply contact the members of this secret society.

A HIDDEN ALLIANCE OF FRIENDS

Impossible? Don't be too sure. For with the method this chapter gives you, you will find friends you never dreamed existed. It will be like belonging to an elite group, a secret society, or magic ring of power. Try to think of it this way.

For if friendship is giving, there is nothing that friends cannot do for each other.

HOME REMODELED LIKE NEW

An elderly couple of my acquaintance, Mr. and Mrs. G., were badly in need of some repairs on their home. Yet they were both retired, living on a small income, and Mr. G. had a bad heart. Clearly, they were in no position to leave their home, which was paid for—and yet they couldn't afford the needed repairs nor do it themselves.

But because they were so well loved in the neighborhood where they had lived for many years, and because of their many past favors for others, all the neighbors—upon hearing of their plight—chipped in and helped make the needed repairs.

It was a magic transformation. Several of the younger men helped put on a new roof. Others gave the house a fresh coat of paint. Twenty-five neighbors chipped in and purchased a new heating system for the house—boiler, hot water heater, and all. They even put in a new patio and barbecue for them.

A NEW FINISHED BASEMENT

Another true story. Shortly after I moved into my new home, I discovered from my neighbors—a close circle of friends, who had all been there since the houses were originally built— that they had all helped each other do certain things, like putting tile on the kitchen walls, laying down linoleum. I noticed that several of the houses had the same log-type ranch fences, and sure enough, they had all helped each other put them in years before.

One neighbor pointed out that even the basement in my own house had been finished with the help of neighbors who still lived nearby. It had a bar, a game room, beautiful closets, and shelves—even a bathroom of its own, with a stall shower, installed by these "unseen" helpers.

I could hardly believe that people could be so friendly to one another, until I came home from work one snowy winter day, and found that the paths, sidewalks, and driveways of my house had been completely shoveled and cleared of snow! Even I, a newcomer, was being quickly and lovingly absorbed by this close circle of friends.

* * * * * *

In another instance, an acquaintance of mine, Claire D., told me how a new addition to her home had "sprung up" like magic. How friends had helped them put up a new two-car garage—with brick frontage, automatic sliding doors, aluminum siding—and even a back patio. Practically every item had been purchased, with the help of these friends, at little or no cost. Yet the garage, patio, and breezeway, when completed, added $12,000 in value to the house!

The examples are seemingly endless.

A MAGIC RING OF POWER

To make and hold a friend, with the Magic Mirror Technique, as described in these pages, is like having a magic golden ring. And to talk to such a friend is often like rubbing a magic ring, to ask for and instantly receive the things you desire. Any *group* of friends is like an actual Magic Ring of Power.

Starting today, make it a point to discuss your problems with your friends—seek their advice, their judgement. They can often see—clearly and correctly—when you, yourself, are too close to the problem to judge what to do correctly, without overly emotional involvement; such as, fear, sadness, anger, unrest, depression, or overexcitement. They can often warn you when you are making the wrong decisions, and urge you on when you are making the right ones. In addition, they may have knowledge or experience, know people, or have needed contacts that you do not possess. You never know what someone can do for you until you discuss matters with him fully.

LONG-LOST SON RETURNS

John P. was in his sixties and newly retired when the thought of his son, whom he hadn't seen in years, began to weigh heavily on him. And yet he had no idea of where his son might be. The boy had left home, at an early age, to seek his fortune—and after several letters, and an occasional visit home, the two had completely lost contact.

But John was a friendly sort, who made friends easily, simply by listening and applying the Magic Mirror Technique. And one day, when a man from the electric company came to read his meter, the two got to talking. One thing led to another, and John got to mentioning his son, in the Merchant Marines, whom he hadn't seen in years.

"You don't say!" the man replied. "I have a neighbor in the Merchant Marines. Maybe he knows your son. I'll ask him for you."

As it turned out, the man's neighbor did not actually know John's son, but *he*, in turn, was able to spread the word among *his* friends.

One day, soon afterwards, the doorbell rang, and there he was, smiling, arms outstretched in greeting—like a vision out of thin air! "Hi, Dad," he said. "I got the word, and here I am. You pulled me to you like a magnet!" he laughed. "Next time, just leave word with the home office, and I'll know where you are."

A STRANGER HANDS HIM $500

Harry G. had an idea for a new business. He got it while painting his house. A new spray process that would enable anyone—man or woman, old or young—to freshen up their homes with a new coat of paint, quickly, easily, with practically no fuss or bother—ten times faster than any method currently in use.

The trouble was, he needed at least $500 to get started, and he had barely $50 to his name. Someone told him about the method (revealed in Chapter 5) for selling stock to obtain needed money, and Harry laughingly decided to give this method a try. Using this method, he decided to spread the word among his friends that he had a fantastic idea for a new business. Revealing only the bare details, he told them he would be willing to cut them in on a portion of the profits, if they would lend him the money he needed. Most of them said it sounded like a crazy idea. Some said they would be glad to help, if they had the spare cash—which they didn't. A few quickly chipped in with $10, $20, and $30 contributions—but it wasn't nearly enough.

But Harry decided to make just one more effort. Using the method revealed in Chapter 5, Psycho-Motion Pictures, he set up a company—using the few dollars contributed by friends—and made a public stock offering. He took out a small newspaper ad, offering shares in his new company, and when he received an inquiry, he would send a letter with complete details.

The response was immediate and overwhelming. He began receiving cash, checks, and money orders from eager investors all over the country, totaling about $5,000—money that was his, interest-free, tax-free, to use any way he saw fit!

Some people even rang his doorbell, out of the clear blue sky, cash in hand, ready to invest in his new business. One man, a wealthy business investor, handed him $500 in cash, saying he had faith in this new idea, and if it worked out, there was more where that came from!

Harry used this money to take several business trips, gathering information and visiting several companies that produced the equipment he needed. He set up shop on a small scale, produced a small number of paint-spray kits which he took to department store buyers and other retail outlets as samples, and promptly signed up orders for several large shipments.

As orders increased, his business grew—until now, almost overnight, Harry, a former low-paid assembly-line worker, is a rich man, receiving ten times as much from his business as he did punching a time-clock in a factory. He has a new home, a new car, a swimming pool of his own, a cabin cruiser, wears the best clothes, eats in the best restaurants, and has plenty of leisure time to enjoy his money. And he owes it all to friends he never knew existed—total strangers—all over the country.

ASK FOR LOVE AND COMPANIONSHIP

Bradford D. bemoaned the fact that he had never had any experience with women. He lived alone, with his mother, and had spent most of his life working, studying, and supporting relatives who were bleeding him white. He was shy and self-conscious about his appearance. Short and skinny, he thought that most girls would—indeed, did—laugh at him and not take him seriously, and so he never even tried.

At 35, he was a lonely, miserable bachelor. At his age, he thought, most girls were either already married or too young for him. It looked hopeless. But Bradford had several married and unmarried friends, where he lived and where he worked, who noticed his sad, listless attitude, and inquired why he was so silent and distant. Gathering up his courage (this was his Supreme Command), he admitted his problem—and asked if they knew any eligible girls. Certainly, they replied. Why not take this or that phone number, call up, and see?

Bradford was greatful for their help—but still a long way from the full self-confidence he needed. But by speaking out—*doing* something—he had set the wheels in motion without even realizing it.

One evening, while he was sitting home, alone, the doorbell suddenly rang—and when he answered it, there were his neighbors, Jack and Helen, and a beautiful young woman they introduced as Elizabeth, Jack's cousin, here for a short visit.

They invited themselves in, in a friendly way, and after a few drinks, insisted that Brad go out with them for dinner and some entertainment. Elizabeth was warm and friendly, and her charm seemed to bring out the best in Bradford. Slowly, he began to gain confidence in himself. Despite the fact that she was so different from him, tall and blonde and very attractive, she seemed interested in everything he had to say. He spent more and more time visiting his neighbors, just to see her.

It broke both their hearts, when the day of her departure arrived. And when he saw her off at the train, tears came to both their eyes. Bradford felt his voice choke as he said his last goodbyes. She would return next summer, but by that time, he was sure, she would have forgotten all about him.

Meanwhile, his friends at the office urged that he go out with them, get out into the world, and see what life is all about. To their surprise, Brad accepted their invitations. There were parties and dancing—Brad learned all the popular steps—and met and dated many attractive, eligible young ladies, who were magnetically drawn to him with his new "aura" of self-confidence and self-assurance.

Partying and wild times, however, were not really in his nature—and his mind kept going back to Elizabeth, and the quiet summer they had spent together. He wrote to her more frequently, praying that she would answer. And each time she did.

When summer finally came again, Bradford and Elizabeth had many things to talk about. Brad told her about his past life, the loneliness, and how she had opened up a new world to him. Elizabeth said he should never think that way again—that he was as handsome and attractive as any man she had ever met, and well-bred, too. Then she confessed that she, also, had had many similar experiences—her handicap being that she had always felt she was too tall. These intimate revelations touched Bradford deeply.

"I guess I'll just wind up an old maid," she sighed.

Bradford turned on her sharply, and said, "Don't ever talk that way. How could you even think it? Why, I'd give my right arm to marry you. If I thought—that is—would you? I mean . . ."

The next words were the most important that Bradford ever spoke. The wedding took place at summer's end. Today they are the happiest couple I know—happy and proud, and not at all ashamed of what they owe to the miraculous gift of friendship.

RECEIVE A SPIRITUAL HEALING

The greatest advantage of sharing with others and becoming part of a close circle of friends is that a small group can pool its psychic resources (remember the wise old saying, "two heads are better than one").

One person may be a little down one week and the others are able to supply the needed lift and inspiration this person needs. Later, another group member may feel a little "out of sorts" and may get just the gentle charge of spiritual power necessary to carry on without depression.

Phillip O., a neighbor of ours, was in just such a state of depression. His problem was his thinning hair. At a relatively young age, 43, he was growing prematurely bald and grey. He felt old before his time. He had trouble getting a job. He was a salesman, and although he had a youthful physique and healthy appearance, his lack of hair made him look older. "I can and will do something about it," Phillip insisted to himself—and this was his Supreme Command. He decided to bring the problem out into the open and discuss it with his friends.

We sat around the barbecue one day, discussing Phillip's problem, and one of our group, a health enthusiast, said that he had read many reports that showed that balding and greying does not have to take place, in many cases—that it can be prevented, and hair can actually be restored, with proper nutrition (and even where baldness is hereditary, hair transplants can bring back luxurious hair growth, permanently).

This encouraged Phillip O. quite a bit, and he leaned forward, to listen with keen interest. The health enthusiast continued. He said that, according to a study by Dr. Pauline Mack of Texas Woman's University, an inadequate mineral intake is responsible for hair loss and other signs of so-called aging, as young as the 40's.

Dr. Mack found that these problems were reversed when such persons were given supplements of mineral-rich wheat germ and brewer's yeast. In addition, the problems of failing eyesight, brittle bones, anemia, senile blindness, and poor memory were also relieved with these mineral foods.

Of course—he continued—other reasons for hair loss include illness, glandular malfunction, scalp infection, tension, and poor blood circulation. For example, a person who is highstrung, nervous, experiences tightening of the blood vessels leading to the scalp. This means that blood cannot get through to nourish hair roots, hair becomes brittle, dies, and falls out.

As for heredity, this neighbor insisted, this is also related to diet. He said that according to a medical doctor, birth defects—such as hair weakness and poor scalp health—are traced to improper dietary habits of the mother. If one is born with a thick shock of hair, he told Phillip O., and keeps it until adulthood, and then somewhere along the way loses it, it is his own doing, his own neglect of proper diet.

REGAINS HAIR GROWTH

All this was of great interest to Phillip O., and he became an avid reader on the subject. He discovered that exercise stimulates the body to produce hormones needed for hair growth. He discovered that *silicon* is an essential mineral for hair growth, but that it is often *taken out* of foods such as bran and wheat germ and flour, by manufacturers.

He read that hair-growing silicon may be obtained from steel-cut oatmeal and unbleached whole wheat products—at most groceries and health food stores. He read about a young man who began aging prematurely, with greying hair, wrinkled skin, a feeble voice, and all the symptoms of very advanced age. His doctor decided to try nutritional therapy—gave him enormous amounts of every known mineral, with large amounts of brewer's yeast and whole wheat germ, and also fresh liver juice. In two months, this man underwent a complete rejuvenation. His wrinkles disappeared! His natural hair color was restored, his missing hair magically regrew! He regained all his youthful pep and energy.

Phillip O. was really excited. He read about another man, past middle age, who had begun to lose most of his hair at 30. What remained turned completely white. Frantically, he tried ointments, heat lamps, massage—everything. All failed. Then he tried giving up highly processed foods for natural foods. He gave up coffee, white sugar, and bread. He used honey, fruit, and other all-natural foods. He starting eating sunflower seeds, about one-half cup for breakfast. Then he tried sunflower seed meal (freshly ground), along with pumpkin seed meal and other natural foods. In a few months, he noticed dark hair at the temples. Then soon nearly half his hair was black. After about 18 months, the once shiny pate developed light fuzz. After 18 months more, hair at the forehead filled in slowly. And still another man, young and bald, starting with just a fringe around the edges and dropped deep back, tried the same method— according to what Phillip read. Bit by bit, his hair slowly began to regrow! Soon, he had a very good growth that could be considered a miracle! His hair had turned grey, but when it started to grow back, the color became dark. This all happened within weeks.

After getting his doctor's okay, Phillip decided to try this method, without any further delay. He stuck to it faithfully, for about two years—at the end of which time, sure enough, his hair had darkened perceptibly, and his once bald pate now boasted a fine growth of hair down the front and across the top. Delighted and convinced that, if continued, his hair would eventually be fully restored, Phillip was worried about only one thing: the time factor. And so he decided to speed matters up a bit by having a professional hair transplant. Once again, by asking around among his friends, he was able to locate a doctor who could do this for him. (You can easily do the same by calling up the local branch of the American Medical Association. They will recommend at least three doctors in your area who specialize in healing any specific ailment you might desire.) Today, Phillip O. has a full, rich, luxurious hair growth that makes him look 20 years younger—a gift of youth that might never have come about without the aid, advice, and encouragement of his good friends.

ARTHRITIS RELIEVED

Another neighbor of ours, Mrs. P., 78, suffered crippling arthritic symptoms. Her fingers were swollen and enlarged at the joints, making it impossible for her to sew and do many of the things she enjoyed doing when she was younger. Her knee was stiff, too, and her painfully inflamed ankle caused her to walk slowly, with a limp.

A wonderful neighbor, and a friend to everyone, Mrs. P. never complained. (Every one of us considers her one of the family, and we all call her grandma.) She always managed to visit all her friends at least once a week. But finally, when the visits slowed down, we all suspected it was her arthritis. When questioned about it closely, she admitted, "My dear, you wouldn't believe the pain."

As it turned out, Mrs. P. didn't believe in medicines and doctors. But when she learned that my own mother—who looked, felt, and acted years younger—was suffering from this very ailment, and that she was under a doctor's care, and when she learned of the wonderful treatments that are available, Mrs. P. became interested. The only trouble was, she felt she could never afford such treatment.

We told her about the free clinics and visiting services that are available in all communities—and through our urging, Mrs. P. availed herself of these services. Today, she no longer winces with pain with every step she takes. She can sew, clean, and even get a wonderful night's sleep. Above all, she loves to work outdoors, tending the flowers and grass, and this she can do without any trouble, to her great delight.

Mrs. P.'s recovery—at her advanced age—was so remarkable, that her next-door-neighbor, Mrs. D. F., who was considerably younger (42) but had been hiding the fact that she was suffering from agonizing arthritic symptoms in the shoulders for years, was also inspired to seek help. (Her case was so bad that her husband had been forced to put in an automatic garage door opener.) Now, thanks to these new wonder drugs, Mrs. D. F. looks, feels, and acts years younger.

FINDS MONEY ON DOORSTEP

Residents of Willow Grove smiled knowingly as they read this item in the *Evening Chronicle*: "Mrs. Thelma Jackson, of 1422 Crescent Boulevard, telephoned the *Chronicle* today to express her heartfelt gratitude to all her friends and neighbors for what they have done for her.

"Mrs. Jackson, whose husband Myron Jackson lies seriously ill of chronic nephritis, made an urgent appeal to our readership for help in obtaining a portable kidney machine. 'It's our only hope,' she explained, in an article that appeared in these pages last Tuesday. Mr. Jackson, a former construction worker, was given six months to live without it.

" 'I needed money badly,' says Mrs. Jackson. 'A kidney machine costs $30,000. My husband hasn't worked in months, and we can't even meet the mortgage payments. So I sent up a silent call for help—lots of it. [This was her Supreme Command.] Then the idea came to me to write a letter to the *Chronicle*.

" 'The response was immediate and automatic. I can't tell you how thankful we are. The next morning (after the article appeared) I found a stack of hundred dollar bills, neatly wrapped in a package by my front door. Who could have done that? I just have no idea. But I've received cards, letters, and telegrams from people all over the county, offering help and support. It's just wonderful—and now it looks as though we'll make it, and then some!'

"Mrs. Jackson and her husband are long-time residents of Willow Grove, and have been active in many church and civic groups. They have three children, Norma, 4, Irene, 8, and Myron Jr., 13."

The Magic Symbol or Seal of Friendship:

Two spirits clasped within a ring of power.

A SPEED-O-MATIC DESIRE-BRINGER—MORE POWERFUL
THAN A BILLION ATOM BOMBS!

The element of telepathy in prayer and group prayer methods cannot be ignored. For who is to say how much the power of silent commands had to do with the results achieved in all these cases? My theory—and, incidentally, it is a theory shared by many—is that it had a great deal to do with them.

When you form a friendship, or a group of friends, your psychic power quite often becomes aligned with theirs. How else can you explain the fact that close friends will often think the same thought simultaneously? How else can you explain the awesome power that brings instantaneous healings in group revival meetings?

From a psychic point of view, a chain is as strong as its weakest link. And a group of friends working together, through prayer, can often generate power which staggers the imagination—power that can literally move mountains—like a Psycho-Command Machine, a Cosmic Mind Machine or Dream Maker that turns dreams to reality, a giant Insta-Magnet, Miracle Magnet, Ideo-meter, or Creato-Matic Machine.

Throughout occult literature there runs the Secret Doctrine of the "hidden power structure"—always a group of people united in prayer. Reese P. Dubin, in his book, *Telecult Power**, reports on just such a group of people, who agreed to unite in prayer, to solve the problems of each of them. (He calls any such group of two or more people a Hidden Brotherhood.)

One member, A. W., a small debt-ridden shopkeeper, received $20,000 in cash, a refund of several thousand dollars from the largest of his creditors, and a tuition-free scholarship for his son—starting the very first week! Another member, Mrs. B., was offered a sum that would take care of the back payments on her home—by a complete stranger. A third member, Mrs. D., began receiving letters from her estranged husband, begging her to return home. A fourth member, Richard G.—a

---

*Reese P. Dubin, *Telecult Power: The Amazing New Way to Psychic and Occult Wonders* (West Nyack, N.Y.: Parker Publishing Company, Inc., 1970).

failing door-to-door salesman—hit a lucky winning streak, and was soon driving around in an air-conditioned Cadillac and living in a $59,000 house, complete with swimming pool and all the modern conveniences.

All of these events apparently occurred as a result of group prayer meetings. One member, Mrs. Julia K., even received a healing, and was able to walk around, completely unassisted—for the first time in years. "During a two-year period," he reports, "this method has been nearly 100% successful... brought estranged family members together, performed seeming miracles in helping the sick, and in making financial gains possible." Somehow it always manages to help.

"Results may come instantly, or after a few days or weeks of accumulated effect," he says, "but results will definitely come, this I promise you, in the direction of your desired goal." "You can ask for anything and expect to receive it," he says.

Kingdon L. Brown* reports very similar findings. In one such group—which discovered, as many others have discovered, for the first time—the power of this method, the total yearly income of the members increased by 35%, two members became happily married, and five significant healings occurred. To get started, he says, your group can consist of up to five people. You should meet once a week, to decide whose problem seems most pressing at the moment. For a relaxing atmosphere, he recommends quiet background music. Light a candle or candles, stand, join hands, and pray that you will be led into the way of Truth.

The actual rituals that you may use, according to Rev. Brown, may be used alone, without a group—although the power is multiplied a hundred, a thousand times over with a group of friends, whose mere presence—like **Cosmic batteries**—can give you a reserve of power.

All the rituals begin with the same two steps: (1) prepare a table to be used as an altar; (2) light a candle and call on your higher spirit messenger (subconscious mind) to assist you in the

---

*Kingdon L. Brown, *Cosmosis: The Technique and Its Use in Daily Living* (West Nyack, N.Y., Parker Publishing Co., Inc., 1971).

creation of whatever it is you seek (love, prosperity, health), and name the person for whom this is to come about. If you are asking for wealth, he says, burn a dollar bill, a check, or some other symbol of wealth as a sacrifice. As the flame dies out, repeat the name of the person for whom this ritual was performed. Dispose of the ashes by placing them in the ground. Repeat this ritual once every 13 days or until prosperity comes into the life of the person for whom the ritual was intended.

The steps are the same for love and health, except that for love, he says, you burn a small part of a garment worn by the person, and as the flame dies out repeat the names of the two people three times. For health, he says, burn anything which is symbolic of the ailment.

*   *   *   *   *   *

All this may sound strange, indeed, to the skeptic or non-believer, and yet it is a method—as valid as any other—for enlisting the power of the subconscious mind through auto-suggestion. Chapter 9 discusses this in greater detail, but for now, suffice it to say that telepathic influence is a reality that scientists are hard-put to explain but are often forced to admit exists.

GIFTS FREE FOR THE ASKING

It costs you nothing to use these secrets of psychic power control, and yet the rewards can be greater than you ever dreamed possible.

In this chapter, we have seen how to command people to do what you want them to do, without uttering a sound! How to bring your mate to you without asking! How to make others work for you secretly, do favors for you, and actually go out of their way to please you!

Keep rereading these chapters, and you'll discover how you can quickly materialize all your fondest dreams, make your dreams come true! ... How to double your wealth and keep it doubling endlessly and automatically! ... How to get one friend and make him get you two more! ... How to keep expanding your circle of friends until you have virtually an entire army of loyal friends and boosters!

Psycho-Command Power #9

INSTA-MAGIC SPELLS
THAT WORK MIRACLES!

If you have been reading these pages carefully, you have sensed your power to command mighty miracles to happen automatically—miracles of wealth, love, and happiness—has increased many times over, and that these miracles are starting to materialize. You may even come to believe that this book—its very words—possess special powers. They do. For they are true words, and true words are alive with power.

In this chapter, you will discover magic spells that work miracles of self-mastery.

HELP FROM THE INVISIBLE WORLD

Earlier in these pages, it was remarked that the human mind is like an invisible being, and in that sense we live in a world of invisible beings upon whom we may call for very real help. That is true.

There is a hidden spirit within each of us called the subconscious mind. It is that hidden side of our consciousness which is amenable to *suggestion*, like a Spirit Messenger, Guardian, or invisible servant who will carry out your orders automatically, without any question. A suggestion, or Psycho-Command, made to this inner self, deep within the body, is like a powerful undercurrent beneath the sea. You are not aware of it. Quietly it works to magically transform your desires into reality.

Suggestion upon one's self, or auto-suggestion, is the voluntary act, and nearly always the involuntary or unconscious act, by which our nervous force is accumulated and concentrated upon an idea, and whose result, or tendency, is to provoke a definite effect.

Auto-suggestion is recognized as the principal cause of many of our actions. It enters into nearly all the circumstances and situations of life. Our designs, our wishes, our joys, are almost always the effect of auto-suggestion or Psycho-Commands. Every Psycho-Command which penetrates to the brain and is perceived by it provokes a reaction and tends to be transformed into an action. If the Psycho-Command is powerful enough and the impression sufficiently deep, the reaction is immediate. An example of such a response would be laughter or sadness. If, on the other hand, the command is merely fleeting and is not repeated, or is only repeated a few times at long intervals, the cerebral reaction will not be sufficiently strong to produce an exterior act, and it may even happen that the impression disappears. If the same Psycho-Command is often repeated, the reaction will be fortified, will increase, and finally, when it has acquired sufficient energy, will effect the act provoked. The accumulated nervous force is abruptly exhausted, and all is in order again, either definitely, or until some future occasion when the same incitations will again affect the nervous system.

In this category may be placed all the diseases of "nervous" origin which may have been occasioned by involuntary or unconscious Psycho-Commands. It has also been thought that an unvarying mode of living and the influence of surroundings may be a factor in causing these morbid ailments and sustaining a malady. This is why a doctor, having exhausted all his resources, will often advise a change of climate or new and different occupations. In all these cases, suggestive treatment may be tried with advantage.

CURES BY TALISMANS AND CHARMS

Religious belief causes cures by auto-suggestion on the part of the invalid, who, possessed of faith, trusts in religion and in the saints or spirits he invokes. Talismans or charms act also by auto-suggestion, and many remedies produce, by auto-suggestion, excellent results. A woman was once cured by *mercurial* treatment, which consisted of the application of a thermometer to the armpit. In the first place, of course, they put it there merely to ascertain her temperature; however, as the sick woman declared that she felt great relief, they continued the application, and she was cured.

Beliefs produce strange effects, due to auto-suggestion. There is, for example, the belief that a rabbit's foot, or horseshoe, or four-leaf clover brings good luck. If your nose bleeds, a saying goes, put a key down the back and it will stop.

We must learn to recognize auto-suggestion, to utilize it in a favorable way—and to fight against it when it interferes with our health or well-being.

THE INVISIBLE CLOCK

Take the case of a traveler who, at a fixed, unalterable hour early next morning must leave by train. On lying down, he says to himself that he must be up and ready to start by such-and-such an hour; he dreams in his sleep; is obsessed by the same thought throughout the night; now and then he wakes up in a fright, rises, looks at the time, and goes back to sleep; his preoccupation is continuous, it persists during his sleep, which it disturbs; there is a fixed idea which has stamped itself on his brain and which remains all night, in spite of his fatigue and his need of rest.

This fixed idea is an auto-suggestion; the labor performed by the mind in order not to miss the time is the result of auto-suggestion; the fact of awakening at the desired hour is a result of auto-suggestion.

But when the same suggestion, by constant repetition, becomes a habit, auto-suggestion ceases to be wearisome or tiring: sleep is calm, tranquil, beneficent; the obsession of rising at a fixed hour disappears; nervous force is preserved; the brain remains passive, and only arouses to action on the awakening, which is effected at the precise moment and is accompanied by a feeling of general well-being, without fatigue or excitement.

This happens when the mind has been educated by the more or less regular repetition of the same act; the idea of awakening only occurs after a certain length of time—like a built-in alarm clock—and does not preoccupy the person, because he has acquired the feeling of certainty that he will wake at the moment fixed by his will.

This example of auto- (or self-) suggestion shows that your conscious mind—your **Master Regulator**—*can govern, control, and give orders* to your deep inner, hidden, *invisible servant,* the subconscious mind, which will dutifully obey.

FREEDOM FROM PAIN*

There are innumerable cases on record of people who are able to introduce pins into their skin without feeling the slightest pain, and the pin-pricks do not bleed. They declare that this freedom from pain occurs *only when they desire it.* It is necessary for them to make this suggestion, for—without it—they would, indeed, feel the pain, and the wounds would bleed.

Others, by simple self-suggestion, are able to speed up or slow down their heartbeat, or the circulation of their blood. And in India, it is common practice for holy men to slow the action of their hearts for long periods of rest and rejuvenation.

REGAINS HEARING

There is a case of an elderly man, John C., we'll call him, who was slightly hard of hearing, and in whose family several

---

*Through laboratory experiments, scientists are now verifying the efficacy of "mind control" (or Psycho-Command) in relieving such illnesses as gastric ulcers, high blood pressure, colitis, certain nervous disorders such as asthma and muscle spasm, insomnia, and to control without drugs cardiac arrhythmias, symptoms of fatigue, migraine, and tension headaches, according to an article in *The New York Times Magazine* of September 12, 1971 by Gay Luce and Erik Peper.

persons had gradually become stone-deaf at the age of 25 or 30, without recognizable cause and not as a result of heredity. This man restored, and has preserved his hearing now for many years, with this Supreme Command, which he administers to himself from time to time at night, at the moment of falling asleep: "There is nothing wrong with me. I am perfectly normal. Many doctors have said so. Surely all their training and experience means something. They can't all be wrong. I, myself, have seen how the imagination can play strange tricks on me. I can be as normal as I want to be. I am as healthy now—healthier, in fact—than I ever was." He uses these words, whenever he feels an onset of the old malady—and it disappears.

SIGHT RESTORED

In the same way, Warren W. regained his sight. A belief in old age had taken hold of him, and his eyesight blurred, along with many other nonorganic symptoms. His doctor assured him that it was only his belief in the "old age devil" that was causing it. And once this was explained—along with the silent method of health affirmations or Supreme Commands—Warren's eyesight cleared, sharpened, and returned to normal.

I recall a similar case in which a neighbor of mine, Roger H., thought he had a detached retina, due to a severe blow. The fear persisted even after the eye was pronounced normal. With this method, his "double vision" cleared, and he has never had a bit of trouble since. At one point, my own father, David J., thought he had astigmatism in both eyes. Everything seemed to jump around and quiver when he looked at it. The optometrists's report: nonorganic. With Psycho-Commands, the condition cleared up entirely.

**HOW SHE WAS FREED FROM A
SO-CALLED EVIL SPIRIT**

Similarly, deep feelings of guilt, hate, resentment, remorse, self-condemnation, anger, and hostility can produce terrifying hallucinations in your mind. As an example of this, Dr. Joseph

Murphy reports* how a woman in San Francisco complained that an evil spirit was constantly annoying her and pouring out vulgarisms, obscenities, and commanding her to violate her sex code, as well as even scratching her at night. After discussing the matter deeply with Dr. Murphy, the woman confessed that she was angry at a close relative—her own anger had been eating away at her, in the form of self-punishment (for she knew she should not be angry). At Dr. Murphy's suggestion, morning, noon, and night, she repeated out loud the words of the great healing and protective 91st Psalm, knowing that as she affirmed these truths, they would neutralize, obliterate, and expunge all evil thoughts from her mind. After about 10 days, the "evil spirit" disappeared—and she has not been bothered by it since.

ARTHRITIC SYMPTOMS RELIEVED

Many symptoms arising from nervous origin seem to have responded to this method. Tension, as we know, can indeed cause a constriction of blood vessels leading to various parts of the body—resulting in very real pain. Gus H. got complete relief for increasing pain in his shoulders, back, and legs. Mrs. M. S., a 43-year-old supermarket cashier who complained of leg pain, was surprised when it disappeared. James McV., a 45-year-old auto mechanic complained of severe backache and stiffness when he got out of bed in the morning and could hardly move. After using this method, he states, "The pain and stiffness are gone," and he can bend freely, take long hikes, and even go swimming. Lydia E., a 52-year-old cosmetics saleslady who tried this technique said that it relieved the soreness and stiffness in her fingers when nothing else seemed to help.

In every case, doctors—who had failed to help—assured these people that nothing could be done medically, since their ailments were caused by a belief that had taken hold of them, and nothing more.

---

*Dr. Joseph Murphy, *Psychic Perception: The Magic of Extrasensory Power* (West Nyack, N.Y.: Parker Publishing Co., Inc., 1971).

ULCER RELIEVED

I, myself, had a very painful bout with ulcers, stomach cramps, terrible heartburn, acid indigestion, and a gnawing pain in the midsection that lasted for nearly ten years, until I learned of this method. The cause and cure rested in my belief in these symptoms, the doctor assured me, and when I learned how to control them with this method—affirming to myself, "Relax and heal, heal and be well," whenever the pain came upon me—I obtained complete relief!

COLITIS SYMPTOMS RELIEVED

Bella S. complained of "ulcerative colitis" that had plagued her for years, with stomach cramps and diarrhea, no matter what she ate. And yet the doctor said the cause and cure lay within her mind. With this method, she obtained fast relief, and has never been bothered with these symptoms since.

HEART SYMPTOMS RELIEVED

Harry G. was on the verge of becoming a "cardiac cripple"—unable to go anywhere or do anything but rest. He was so short of breath so much of the time that he couldn't walk a half block without sheer exhaustion. He also noticed increasing dizziness. The doctor assured him it was the mere fact that cardiac trouble ran in his family that had seized him, nothing more. And he showed Harry this method. Magically, he was able to live again! Soon he was able to resume all his former activities without any pain or worry.

HIGH BLOOD PRESSURE RELIEVED

Ann B. complained of "high blood pressure." She had frequent throbbing "migraine" headaches (most severe in early morning), dizziness, and shortness of breath. This made her tired, nervous, and irritable. The doctor told her there was no organic cause for this and showed her this method. The dizziness and shortness of breath disappeared. Her blood pressure returned to normal—and she felt better, more relaxed and refreshed than she had in years.

INSTA-MAGIC SPELLS THAT WORK
MIRACLES OF SELF-MASTERY

It is clear, therefore, that by auto-suggestive action we can influence our whole organism—have a psychic healing; relieve pain; restore youthful health and vitality; even extend the prime of life; and actually fight off diseases of middle and old age in many cases!

Auto-suggestion is best practiced while awaiting natural sleep; for during sleep the inner mind takes over and works, automatically, on the ideas last submitted to it by the conscious mind.

You may have a choice to make, or a problem that calls for knowledge that you do not possess. At this time, you should submit your problem to your subconscious mind.

In slumber, your conscious mind withdraws, so to speak, and your inner mind takes over. Your inner or subconscious mind has access to all the knowledge that has ever been received by you—even long-forgotten memories. It is such a vast storehouse of information, that it has often been referred to as the Universal Mind, comparing it with the All-Seeing, All-Knowing, All-Powerful Cosmic Mind. Many believe, in fact that the two are directly linked; that all our minds are really the Master's Mind in miniature, and that each of us actually carries a small part of God around with us all day.*

"CAPTURED GENIE" REVEALS ALL

If, just before falling asleep, you have pondered deeply over your problem, examining it from every angle, gathering all of its details together clearly—your subconscious mind—whose power

---

*Sigmund Freud, in a sense captured this "magic genie," the subconscious, made it reveal its secrets to him, and we owe much of our knowledge on this subject to his vast writings. Considered a "mad scientist" by many in his day—many of his theories have been proven correct.

you are discovering and harnessing for the first time, like a captured genie—will take these facts, put them together for you automatically, and come up with the solution. Upon awakening, this solution will be revealed to you.

Or, if it is something you just wish to remember—like the man who just wanted to get up on time—you may submit this problem to your subconscious mind. Quietly it works, while you slumber, to retain this information, and bring it to the surface of your consciousness upon awakening. The child who, before sleeping, repeats the lesson he must know on the following day, uses, without being aware of it, the same process.

NIGHT BRINGS COUNSEL

Tell your invisible servant—your inner mind—which will work for you tirelessly during sleep, to help you in this matter, and show you how you may achieve more happiness, or whatever it is you desire.

There is a proverb, "Night brings counsel," which is a very true saying, because it is a recognized fact that many important decisions are arrived at after sleeping on them. Upon awakening, details and minor aspects of the question stand out much more clearly and precisely.

YOUR MENTAL BROWNIES

It is the same process described by Robert Louis Stevenson, author of *Treasure Island, Dr. Jekyll and Mr. Hyde, A Child's Garden of Verses,* and many other favorites, when he said, "My Mental Brownies, God bless them, do one half my work for me when I am asleep, and in all probability do the other half when I am awake."

Students know that to read a lesson once or twice at night, before going to sleep, is often enough to enable them to repeat it the following day. There are certain persons who are their own alarm clocks; it is enough for them to think, on going to bed, of the hour at which they wish to get up, for them to awaken at that hour. Often, sleep will completely dissolve a pain or discomfort somewhere in the body, if one takes care to will firmly that it must disappear. Upon awakening the next morning, one is agreeably surprised to find the pain gone.

NOW! CALL UPON THE MYSTIC POWERS WITH THESE "SECRET SPELLS" AND INSTANTLY ENJOY A WONDERFUL NEW LIFE!

The mechanism being known, it is therefore easy when in bed, without loss of time, to impress upon one's self the desired idea, in accordance with the rules of auto-suggestion. For instance, when we want to rid ourselves of a bad habit, we must fix our mind upon the quality we wish to develop. Closing the eyes, we think for five minutes of the advantages to be gained, advantages we must make ourselves believe we already partially possess. Then, mentally say to yourself: "*I shall do so; I shall put an end to such and such a thing,*" endeavoring to the utmost to determine very precisely what it is you will do and how you will do it. This is your Supreme Command. Or, you may concentrate on any of the Cyclotrons—or hypnotic symbols, such as Fig. A—or Psycho-Motion Pictures in this book, while visualizing or determining your desire.

Repeat this several times under the same conditions, and afterwards, abandoning pure auto-suggestion in order to think only of the advantages to be gained, fix your mind upon going to sleep, which will follow very soon.

Fig. A

The process described above may be usefully employed to solve problems, develop a photographic steel-shutter memory, rout nagging pains, regain sexual vitality, master new skills like lightning, relieve insomnia, and much more.

LOSE WEIGHT WITHOUT DIETING

Psycho-Command may even be used to lose weight without dieting—in the conventional sense. By automatically conditioning the mind to avoid *overeating* of fattening and starchy foods, you can shed pound after pound of ugly, unwanted fat, trim the abdomen, firm the hips, get rid of a big, bulging waistline, and yet eat all you want—even sweets (such as fresh fruits and fruit candies)—without counting calories.

I know because I did it myself, with this method—losing 25 pounds in less than a month. Another user, Bob E., had a burly, middle-aged paunch, although he was still a relatively young man. Once he discovered this method, however, the pounds melted away with astonishing speed. Almost overnight, it seemed, he was slim and dapper, wearing the latest young men's styles. Where all other methods had failed (even diet clubs)—this one worked, in just a few short weeks. Now 30 pounds lighter, he is obviously pleased with his image in the mirror, and the fit of his clothes.

REGAIN HAIR GROWTH

As Dr. Samuel Homola notes*—"There are some dermatologists who say that baldness occurs when the scalp becomes so tight that the circulation of blood to the hair roots is restricted. The hair simply falls out from lack of adequate nourishment." Psycho-Command can relax the body, relieve tension, and in so doing help increase healthy circulation.

This method of Psycho-Command to the inner mind was reportedly used by a young man who had tension headaches that were so severe they were literally squeezing the hair out of

---

*Samuel Homola, D.C., *Secrets of Naturally Youthful Health and Vitality* (West Nyack, N. Y.: Parker Publishing Co., Inc., 1971).

his head. With this method, his headaches vanished and his hair resumed a luxuriant growth. Whenever he felt a tension headache coming on, he would simply sit back, relax, and repeat the Supreme Command, "Relax and heal . . . Relax and heal." If tension is your problem, along with non-male pattern baldness, Psycho-Command may help you, too.

MAKE WRINKLES DISAPPEAR

Charles Fillmore was nearing the age of 50, when he wrote: "About three years ago, the belief in old age began to take hold of me . . . I began to get wrinkled and grey, my knees tottered, and a great weakness came over me." With this method, however, he told his inner mind "that I would never submit to the old age devil, that I was determined never to give in. Gradually I felt a new life current coming up . . . a faint little stream at first . . . . Now it is growing by leaps and bounds. My cheeks have filled out, the wrinkles and crow's feet are gone, and I actually feel like the boy that I am." Later, at the age of 65, Mr. Fillmore went through an illness so serious that doctors did not see how he could survive. Yet he came out of it with renewed vigor, and lived another 30 years.*

FINDING LOST OBJECTS

One very practical use to which this power may be put is in the finding of lost objects—keys, photos, documents, money, and other valuables—that may have been mislaid or forgotten. Very often, the power of the subconscious mind, when invoked this way—prior to sleep—will lead to the sudden realization, the next day, of where it may be found. And an "inner voice" or "flash of insight" will lead you directly to it.

This is clearly explained by Reese P. Dubin, in his book, *Telecult Power*†: "There is an extraordinary phenomenon in

---

The Household of Faith, by James Dillet Freeman (reported by Catherine Ponder, in *The Dynamic Laws of Healing*, Parker Publishing Co., Inc., West Nyack, N. Y., 1966).

†Reese P. Dubin, *Telecult Power: The Amazing New Way to Psychic and Occult Wonders* (West Nyack, N.Y.: Parker Publishing Company, Inc., 1970).

psychology called peripheral vision. It means that we see things out of the corners of our eyes without realizing it. (The same thing happens with hearing.) These impressions escape us merely because we were concentrating on something else at the time, but they enter our minds just the same—our subconscious minds—and can be recalled, either accidentally or on purpose."

For example, "A sight or sound not consciously perceived by you three days ago, because your attention was fixed on something else at the time, *was* actually received by you and passed directly into your subconscious mind," he says. "Now, three days later, when your conscious mind is not busily engaged in other matters, this memory pops into your mind."

With this method of finding lost objects, the mind is deliberately told to set about the task of remembering exactly where the object is. This is done prior to sleep, so that the mind will have nothing else to do but turn this over and over, subconsciously, during the night. It may also be accomplished in the waking state, during periods of complete—or deep relaxation—known as daydreaming.

SHE FINDS VALUABLE DOCUMENTS

A friend of mine, Mrs. Alma J., is especially adept at using this technique. "All I do," she says, "is put the problem up to my subconscious mind. I don't concentrate on it *consciously*, but just go into a sort of dreamlike reverie, staring at the wall, perhaps, and thinking of nothing in particular. After a while, I can *see* exactly where it is and go directly to (the lost object)."

It is interesting to note, however, that Mrs. J. also insists that this method enables her to "see" the location of objects about which she has *no prior knowledge*. This is called clairvoyance and may be an added benefit for you in using this method. "I can always go directly to the object," she says.

Once, for example, Mrs. J. and her father were greatly distressed to discover some valuable bonds were missing. The bonds together with several other documents had been put aside years ago, when it was thought that they were worthless. Now, however, they were worth approximately $1,000—if cashed quickly—and the whole family was in an uproar. Where could they be?

Mrs. J. decided that this case was no different from all the others she had been able to solve with this method. So she put the problem up to her inner mind, sat down, relaxed, and let her conscious mind go blank, in a kind of dreamlike reverie. In a matter of minutes, in this dreamlike state—amidst the stream of thoughts that flowed past her mind—she suddenly remembered a packet of papers on the top shelf of the closet in her daughter's room. A quick investigation revealed that, true to the law, there were the bonds, exactly where her father had left them years before!

MONEY APPEARS ALL OVER
HIS ENTIRE HOUSE!

Robert E. had a habit of stashing odd sums of money around the house. The only trouble was, he was always forgetting where he stashed it. Under the rug? Behind a picture? Under a seat cushion? A mattress? Inside a light fixture? Under his shirts in the drawer? The question "Where?" continually plagued him—especially when he used up all his cash, and couldn't find any more, as often happened.

It bothered him; that is, until he discovered this method. Now, all he does is put the problem up to his "mental brownies," and this secret leads him straight to the various hiding places—$25, $15, $10, $50—and he is never short of cash.

PHOTOGRAPH COMES ALIVE—PEOPLE IN IT
LEAD HER TO BURIED TREASURE!

Dorothy B. was flipping through an album of old photographs, when she suddenly came across a picture of her brother and some friends, as children, at play, that caught her attention. There was "something" odd about that picture—something strange—she couldn't quite remember.

Try as she might, she couldn't remember. It made her restless and uneasy. Finally, she put the problem up to her subconscious mind with the method of Supreme Commands just shown. True to the law, her inner mind had not forgotten—

indeed, never forgets anything—and that night, while sleeping, the scene of the photograph appeared, once again, in her dreams.

In the dream, her brother and his friends were playing in the backyard of their old home in New Haven, Connecticut. She was only four at the time, watching—while her brother and his friends were playing Treasure Island. They laughingly chose up sides—one side the pirates, the other buccaneers. And her brother hid while the pirates buried the "treasure." Then, after a mock battle, her brother proceeded to dig for the buried treasure. Instead of finding it, however—he uncovered an old tin can filled with money!

They decided, however, that the money was evil, and that there must be a curse on it—as 10-year-olds will—and quickly buried it again, never mentioning it to a soul.

Upon awakening, Dorothy decided to check this out. She drove out to her parent's house in New Haven. From the photograph, she was able to tell exactly where they had been playing, and pace off the distance of the treasure from her dream. A few shovelfuls of dirt—and suddenly there it was! Exactly as it was in her dream! Exactly as it had been for 20 years—and longer. It contained $840 in $100 and $20 bills!

* * * * * *

There is nothing that you cannot have, once you call upon the mighty servant of your subconscious mind with these magic spells. This secret can give you magnetic personal power; it can solve problems for you; it can lead you to the path of true happiness—if you will only learn to call upon it.

It can make you a Mental Wizard—100 times as smart as you are now—almost overnight! It can enable you to read anything 1,000 times faster than you can read today. Absorb facts like a sponge—and repeat them almost word for word years later! Skim through a book in minutes! Dazzle others with your memory! Automatically amaze people by recalling exact conversations you had with them months before! Win new friends, impress superiors, by remembering details ordinary people completely forget!

It can help you flash through math, business, financial problems that have you stumped today, with your amazing new powers of concentration. Help you quickly understand things that completely mystify most people, things like statistics, balance sheets, profit and loss, even with little or no training. You'll find many problems half solve themselves. It can give you incredible new powers of making and handling money, predicting the stock market, running a business, setting up a budget, making one dollar do the work of ten.

It can give you a power-packed vocabulary—give you the words you need—overnight, simply by looking them up and remembering them, once and for all, without ever looking at a dictionary again. You'll automatically understand hundreds of new words—"smart" words that make people stop and listen to you. Whiz right through dozens of make-or-break tests. . .license tests. . .promotion tests. . .break any test wide open. . .without misspelling a single word. You'll have every fact you need, right at your fingertips, because your thoughts will organize themselves automatically, the night before! And you'll be able to write business letters and reports that set you head and shoulders above the crowd.

You'll out-think others when you have to—tower over them in judgment. . .and do it all, not by struggling through dreary textbooks. . .not by memorizing useless theories—but simply by putting your untapped MENTAL POWERS to work, today!

Psycho-Command Power #10

CREATING FUTURE EVENTS

It is hoped that in the reading of these pages, you will have come to understand that to a very great extent, the future of your choice is up to you.

Only you can decide how much of the good things in life you want. And only you can decide whether you will really use the techniques, methods, and steps revealed in this book to get them. They are all here, waiting for you to put them into action! Do they work? Most assuredly. They can work beyond your wildest dreams!

ALL HIS DESIRES CAME TRUE
THROUGH PSYCHO-COMMAND POWER

Psycho-Command *can* change your life instantly, from the very moment you let it work for you. Here is a typical example of how one man, Gordon D., used this power to make all his dreams come true. In a recent conversation, he told me:

"I wanted an income of $25,000 a year—despite the fact that I had no special training or abilities—and

I received it. I wanted a spacious new home of my own, with all the modern conveniences—despite the fact that I came from the poor side of the tracks—and I received them. I wanted nothing less than a brand-new yellow Cadillac convertible—even though I had never owned a car—and I received it. I *knew* some day I'd be living in the swankiest part of town, and I am! I *knew* that I would meet and marry a beautiful woman, who would bear me three lovely children, and that our life together would be a heaven on earth. *And all these things happened!* Call it magic or anything else you wish, but this technique has really worked for me. And if it worked for me, it can work for anybody!"

WEALTH, LOVE, AND POWER
CAN BE YOURS

Think about that. "If it can work for me, it can work for anybody." The words of a man who knew poverty, failure, and despair, urging you to try this method and let it work for you.

> **If in the past you have not used this power, that is too bad—as far as the past is concerned—but it is not too late! You can start NOW. What more are you waiting for? God can do for you only what you allow Him to do through you, but if you will do your part, He can use you as a channel for unlimited power and good.**

Confidence is the key. Believe and you shall receive. Believe, and you shall have it—easily and automatically—whatever it is you desire. Let "Yes, I believe!" be your Supreme Command, calling into action your subconscious mind. In this manner, you may actually raise your I.Q.—raise it 50 to 100 points, by actual scientific tests, through belief alone! Starting in just one evening!

In one famous experiment, ordinary and even below average students—failures, dropouts, 5-percenters, tne bottom of the barrel—were placed in a special class, called "college prep" because of their high I.Q.s, or so they were told. And, thinking they were smarter, their minds began to act with full, roaring genius power. Their test scores zoomed to fantastic new highs! Their I.Q.s rocketed an incredible 25%—putting them in the genius class—simply because they thought they were geniuses!

And out of this class, a hopeless "failure" of a boy, Gene C., we'll call him, went on to become a famous movie producer— despite the fact that he had never done or said anything before to show he had this talent, and was previously even a failure with girls. Another student, James K., went on to become a million- aire banker and investor—although previously, he couldn't even add a grocery list. Still another student, Tanja D.—who could barely read when she entered the class, went on to become a college English instructor, and has written many wonderful books and articles that have brought her wide acclaim!

Even among adults, this technique has proved all-powerful. . . enabling a 45-year-old businessman, whose restaurant was badly in the red, with creditors threatening to foreclose, to quickly come up with a great new plan to get the credit he needed and and increase sales 100%. Today this man, Michael W., owns a chain of restaurants, each bearing his name, and bringing him an automatic income of $100,000 a year! Yet he spends just 3 days a week supervising them!

Samuel B., owner of a small textile company, was on the verge of shutting down his service department, because the fig- ures showed it was losing $35,000 a year. However, putting the problem up to his subconscious mind, he soon discovered a plan that showed this department could actually make $20,000 a year profit—and it quickly became one of his most lucrative operations!

The pages of history are filled with the names of men you would have written off as failures, who held onto their faith— and when their chance came, they were ready and seized it. The records of business are crowded with the names of middle-aged nobodies—failures—who saw their chance, seized it, and became rich: rich in love, rich in money, rich in power, and in spiritual health.

Psycho-Command can be—indeed *is*—just such a chance for you. Seize it and use it now!